Patrick Cour

A Guide

by Thomas D. Perry

ISBN: 1442160373
EAN-13: 9781442160378
Library of Congress Control Number: 2009904241

Laurel Hill Publishing
P. O. Box 11
4443 Ararat Highway
Ararat, VA 24053
www.freestateofpatrick.com
freestateofpatrick@yahoo.com

Cover photo is the home of Charles B. Ross, built in 1828, who was the son of Civil War soldier David Lee Ross near Woolwine, Virginia. Title page photo is the Reynolds Homestead, the Rock Spring, home tobacco magnet R. J. Reynolds in Critz, Virginia.

For Caroline Susan "Carrie Sue" Bondurant Culler
One of those interviewed and at this writing celebrating her one
hundredth year.

"Patrick County citizens have as much as they might appear to lack: resourcefulness, a regard for the ironies and uncertainties of the life, a deep appreciation of the land and for family, dignity, playfulness, independence and evident suspicion of prescriptive notions for their lives and livelihoods. In Virginia's political circles the county is known with good reason as the Free State of Patrick." --- Frank Adams

"Patrick County's a way of life, a way of thinking. It's independent…The land is the heart and soul of Patrick County. It's etched into the consciousness of every native of Patrick County. It's part of their waking up, and their day and their going back to bed. Their feeling for it, their love of it motivates them. Whether for greed, whether for a generous thought, it all goes back to the land. The shape of the county, the woods, the rivers, streams, it's almost a mystical communication with it." -- Ruth Jean Bolt

"I just like the idea of leaving a little old time stuff behind." – Cary Ayers

Also by Thomas D. Perry

Ascent To Glory: The Genealogy of J. E. B. Stuart

The Free State of Patrick:
Patrick County Virginia In The Civil War

J. E. B. Stuart's Birthplace: The History of the Laurel Hill Farm

Images of America: Patrick County Virginia

Images of America: Henry County Virginia

Then and Now: Patrick County Virginia

Notes From The Free State Of Patrick:
Patrick County, Virginia and Regional History

God's Will Be Done: The Christian Life of J. E. B. Stuart

J. E. B. Stuart's Birthplace: A Guide For Educators and Visitors

Visit www.freestateofpatrick.com for more information

Table of Contents

Introduction   7
Using Materials At Virginia Tech   11
Using Materials At The Patrick County Branch Library   15
Interviews   17
Abstracts   21
Interview Name and Subject Index   27

About Tom Perry

J. E. B. Stuart's biographer Emory Thomas describes Tom Perry as "a fine and generous gentleman who grew up near Laurel Hill, where Stuart grew up, has founded J. E. B. Stuart Birthplace and attracted considerable interest in the preservation of Laurel Hill. He has started a symposium series about aspects of Stuart's life to sustain interest in Stuart beyond Ararat, Virginia." Perry holds a BA in History from Virginia Tech in 1983. Tom started the J. E. B. Stuart Birthplace Preservation Trust, Inc. in 1990. The non-profit organization preserved 75 acres of the Stuart property including the house site where James Ewell Brown Stuart was born on February 6, 1833. Perry wrote the eight interpretive signs about Laurel Hill's history along with the Virginia Civil War Trails sign and the new Virginia Historical Highway Marker in 2002. He spent many years researching traveling all over the nation to find Stuart materials including two trips across the Mississippi River to visit nearly every place "Jeb" Stuart served in the United States Army (1854-1861). He continues his work to preserve Stuart's Birthplace producing the Laurel Hill Teacher's Guide for educators and the Laurel Hill Reference Guide for groups and the organization to share his lifetime of research on the only preserved site in the nation relating to the birthplace and boyhood home of James Ewell Brown Stuart. Tom can be seen on Virginia Public Television's Forgotten Battlefields: The Civil War in Southwest Virginia with his mentor noted Civil War Historian Dr. James I. Robertson, Jr. Perry has begun a collection of papers relating to Stuart and Patrick County history in the Special Collections Department of the Carol M. Newman Library at Virginia Tech under the auspices of the Virginia Center For Civil War Studies. He is the author of over a dozen books. In 2004, Perry began the Free State Of Patrick Internet History Group, which has become the largest historical organization in the area with over 500 members. It covers Patrick County Virginia and regional history. Tom produces a monthly email newsletter about regional history entitled Notes From The Free State of Patrick that goes from his website www.freestateofpatrick.com.

Introduction

"It was the collection of a whole volume of life; the lives lived by Patrick Countians; it was memories, voices, dreams, stories, captured on the modern day miracle of tape."
-- Nancy Lindsey

Frank Adams describes Patrick County, Virginia, where "Appalachia meets Piedmont." The purpose of this guide is to reawaken interest in a forgotten resource on Patrick County history. This guide gives the names of those interviewed along with information such as the interviewer and date of the interviews and whether transcriptions are available. The indexes for subject and name are included for the first time. I transcribed the subject indexes from 3x5 cards located in three boxes at Virginia Tech. Virginia Tech Reference Librarian Dorothy McCombs, whom I knew in college, transcribed from a previous guide compiled by Dorothy McCombs. Amy Elizabeth Snyder typed and combined both indexes for this guide. Special Thanks to Joyce Nester and John Jackson, Special Collections Librarians at Virginia Tech for their assistance during the chaos of construction at Virginia Tech.

One of those interviewed stated, "I wanted the children of Patrick County to know how we lived back then…if somebody doesn't do something they'll never know." This explains why I took on this project because I was concerned that a great source of Patrick County history was forgotten and not easy to use in the best case. It gives us a remarkable snapshot of time in the early 1980s that I believe future generations will appreciate it if this material is used, but "if somebody doesn't do something they'll never know." It is my hope an increased awareness of the contents of this collection will increase interest to finish the transcribing and digitalize the recordings for preservation in the future. At present, less than half of the tapes are transcribed.

The Patrick County Oral History Project or it's official title Patrick County: Continuity and Change in a Rural Community began in February 1979 at an informal discussion about doing oral history in Patrick County and evolved into the project between the Patrick County Branch of the Blue Ridge Regional Library and Reynolds Homestead's Continuing Education Center. The resulting 202 cassettes containing 102 interviews of over 300 hours partially transcribed reside in the Patrick County Branch of the Blue Ridge Regional Library and the Special Collections Department of the Carol M. Newman Library at Virginia Tech.

The project resulted in a film Up and Down Those Roads in 1982 directed and written by Elizabeth Fine with cinematography by Jerry Scheeler. Narrated by Carl Dehart, the documentary features Patrick Countians Ruth Jane Bolt, Jim Shelor, Lynn Foddrell, Posey Foddrell, John D. Hooker, Dorn Spangler, students at Meadows of Dan Elementary School and others. Slide programs and a guide to library materials were produced. This material resides in the Special Collections at Virginia Tech. A more detailed description of the holdings follows in this guide.

Materials from the guide to this collection follow at the end of this document. A grant from the National Endowment for the Humanities sponsored by the Patrick County Branch of the Blue Ridge Regional Library and Virginia Tech through the Reynolds Homestead titled "The Free State of Patrick: The County and It's People" provided three years of funding "To engage Patrick County's adults in recording and preserving a history of the county. To increase community use of the humanities resources of the library and the Reynolds Homestead. To provide primary materials for future research."

The following individuals and their organizations were involved in the Patrick County Project. The Advisory Committee consisted of the following: Betty M. Ragsdale, Director of the Blue Ridge Regional Library; David D. Britt, Director of the Reynolds Homestead; Douglas F. Perry, Librarian Patrick County Branch of the Blue Ridge Regional Library; Ann H. Eastman, Assistant to Dean of the College of Arts and Sciences at Virginia Tech; E. Scott Geller, Professor of Psychology at Virginia Tech; Crandall Shifflett, Professor of History at Virginia Tech; Jean H. Speer, Professor of Communication at Virginia Tech; JoAnn Boles, Professor of Clothing, Textiles and Related Arts at Virginia Tech; Roddy Moore, Director of the Blue Ridge Institute at Ferrum College; Peter Hartman, Assistant Director of the Blue Ridge Institute at Ferrum College; Mary R. Britt, Project Director.

The Patrick County Advisory Committee consisted of the following: Lady Louise Clark, Chairman; Joanne Alexander, Lawrence Bolt, David Britt, Doris Brown, Walter Clark, Anita Cox, Ann H. Eastman, Margaret D. Ericson, Lucille Garrett, Linda Hopkins, Arlene Keith, Mitty McCarthy, Dorothy McCombs, Phyllis Moore, Daisy Pendleton, Joan Pfeifer, James Plaster, John Reynolds, Clay Shelor, Glenna Shelor, Leslie Shelor, Dorothy Shough, Jean H. Speer, Lynn Terry, Joanne Thomas, Claudette Thompson, Donald Welsh, Betty M. Woodridge, Meadows of Dan Elementary School, Trinity Church of God.

Transcribers for the Patrick County Oral History Project were Sara Mabe, Carol Jortner, Beth J. Newman, Dot R. Shough and Freda Belcher. Others involved included: Elizabeth C. Fine, Folklorist at Virginia Tech; Dorothy McCombs, Librarian at Virginia Tech; Jean H. Speer, Senior Folklorist at Virginia Tech; Betty M. Ragsdale, Blue Ridge Regional Library; Margaret D. Ericson, Donald Welsh of the Patrick County Branch

Interviewers were Joanne Alexander, Doris Brown, Anita Cox, Margaret D. Ericson, Phyllis Moore, Daisy Pendleton, Joan Pfeifer, Leslie Shelor, Lynn Terry, Claudette Thompson, Walter E. Clark, Lucille Garrett, Linda Hopkins, Arlene Keith, Mitty McCarthy, James Plaster, John Reynolds and Joanne Thomas.

Groups interviewed included: Hardin Reynolds Elementary School Students: Cheryl Bingman, Jeff Coleman, Greta Cooper, Kenneth Hairston, Ronnie Hopkins, Glen Joyce, Charles Murphy, Denise Penn, Eugene Reynolds, Billy Stone, Thomas Trent, Tammy Watkins; Mary Horn Walker: Marie Goad, Edna Hazelwood, Goldier McAlexander, Gloria Bowman, Karen Walter, Ann Cassell, Millie Hubbard, Ruth Hill; New Hope Church Quilters: Carol Chaney, Rosie Cannady, Nellie Foley, Esther Shough, Mozelle Rorrer, Lee Wilson, Mary Watson, Mary Bowder, Linda Lawless, Gladys Cannady; Patrick County PEP Students: Nathan Biggs, Ann Blackard, Tommy Brammer, Lee Clark, Pinky Clark, Gary Corns, Margaret DeHart, Darren Diggs, Lisa Foley, Sharon Foley, Richard Garraputa, Sarah Hand, Wayne Hatcher, Mark Hopkins, Barry Brown, Barry Hutchens, Tammy Hutchens, Barry Knowles, Ryan Lankford, Jeff Love, Jason Martin, Joe Mills, Clary Shelor, Denise Stanley, Woody Walker, Barry Wood, Alfredo Santibanez; Smith River Boys: Calvin Pendleton, J.A. Midkiff, Clarice Shelor, Jesse Shelor Cruise Howell; Stuart Elementary School Sixth and Seventh Grade Students: Rene Kodenski, Leslie Goad, Elaine Bowman, Andy Shelton, Robbie Mitchell, Joey Lindsey, Mike Hiatt, Tracy Turman, David Hill, Michelle Spence; Woolwine Elementary School Students: Nathan Biggs, Ann Blackburn, Tommy Brammer, Lee Clark, Pinky Clark, Gary Corns, Margaret Dehart, Darren Diggs, Lisa Foley, Sharon Foley, Richard Garraputa, Sarah Haud, Wayne Hatcher, Mark Hopkins, Barry Brown, Barry Hutchens, Tammy Hutchens, Barry Knowles, Ryan Lankford, Jeff Love, Jason Martin, Joe Mills, Clay Shelor, Denise Stanley, Woody Walker, Barry Wood, Alfredo Santibanez (Chilean Exchange Student).

Caroline Susan Bondurant Culler "Carrie Sue" celebrated her one hundredth birthday in 2009. She was one of those interviewed for the Patrick County Oral History Project.

USING MATERIALS AT VIRGINIA TECH

The materials of the Patrick County Project are available in the Special Collections Department of the Carol M. Newman Library at Virginia Tech. Six Volumes of Transcriptions from the tapes are available at Virginia Tech along with the Patrick County Branch, Martinsville Branch and Bassett Historical Center of the Blue Ridge Regional Library.

Please note to listen to the tapes you must order the collection from storage, which takes at least two days to arrive in the Special Collections Department. Listening to reel-to-reel tapes is not possible at present, but equipment to listen to the cassettes is available in Blacksburg. Please contact Special Collections about requesting at specref@vt.edu or (540) 231-6308

Internet Links

Link to Virginia Tech's Online Library Catalog (Addison)
http://addison.lib.vt.edu/english/filter.vtls-basic.html
Link to Special Collections at Virginia Tech
http://spec.lib.vt.edu
Location and Hours of Special Collections at Virginia Tech
http://spec.lib.vt.edu/specgen.html#inf1
Other information for visitors to Special Collections
http://spec.lib.vt.edu/visitors.html

Printed materials at Virginia Tech relating to the oral history project.

F232 P3 P37 1983
The Patrick County Project oral history collection: in the Special Collections Division, University Libraries, Virginia Polytechnic Institute and State University: A Guide. Compiled by Dorothy McCombs. (Also available at the Patrick County Branch, Martinsville Branch and the Bassett Historical Center of the Blue Ridge Regional Library.)

F226 M36
The Appalachian region of Virginia: A Guide to library materials. Compiled by Dorothy McCombs. (Also available at the Patrick County Branch and the Bassett Historical Center of the Blue Ridge Regional Library.)

Ms83-007 Patrick County Project oral history collection, 1980-1982 [manuscript].

Listing of Boxes at Virginia Tech

Box 1 Cassette Tapes
      Box 1 Ayers - J. Myron Clark
      Box 2 Clark, L.- Culler C.
      Box 3 East G. - Hall D.
      Box 5 Hopkins B. – Houchins M.
      Box 6 Howell R. – Mayo Mountain Singers
      Box 7 Mitchell – Pendleton

Box 2 Cassette Tapes
      Box 4 Hall P. – Hooker J.
      Box 8 Penn B. – Roberson W.
      Box 9 Shelor B. – Slate S.
      Box 10 Spangler C. – Terry N.
      Box 11 Thomas J. – Weaver N.
      Box 12 Williams D. – Worley L.
      Box 13 Reel to Reel Tapes
      Ruth Jean Bolt – Elder Bennie Clifton.
      Box 13a Reel to Reel Tapes
      Fred Clifton – Oscar Harris.
      Box 13b Reel to Reel Tapes
      E. McAlexander – Houchins.
      Box 14a Reel to Reel Tapes
      Bertie Shelor – M. Thompson.
      Box 14b Reel to Reel Tapes
      Trinity – Lucy T. Worley

Box 15
120 Folders from interviews including: Biographical Data Sheets, Tape Logs, Releases, and Field Notes for participants.

Box 16 Six Volumes of Transcripts of one-half of the interviews

Box 17 Subject Index A – E
(Please note these indexes are on 3x5 cards and have been transcribed in this guide).

Box 17a Subject Index F – Q
Box 17b Subject Index R – Z
Box 18a Patrick County Project Posters and two copies of the film.

Box 18b (Box 10)
C. L. Spangler and N. R. Terry reel to reel tapes
Slide programs with audiotapes that include the following:
Hard Times by John Reynolds.
Making a Living in Early Patrick County by John Reynolds.
Community Life by Mary Britt.
Growing Up in Patrick County by Crandall Shifflett.
Leaving A Little Old Time Stuff Behind by Jean Speer.
Photos: Subjects include Clark Brothers Store, Patrick County
Courthouse, Patrick Springs Hotel, Civil War Veterans Reunions,
Claudette Thompson interviewing Fred Clifton, John Reynolds, Jean
Speer, Mary Britt, Elizabeth Fine, Buddy Pendleton, Margaret Donelion,
Foddrell Family, Cary Ayers and David Britt.
Slides: Subject include John and Novella Handy, Arlene Keith, Addie
Wood, Karen Thompson, Vesta Community Potluck Dinner, Mrs. Turner
"Jarring the Comb," Dancing Sam and Fred Clifton, Jim Shelor and
daughters, Ammon Sears and Carl Dehart, Coy Yeatts, Phipps Bourne
(Woodworking and Blacksmithing at Mabry Mill), The Foddrells
(Turner, Allie, Posey, Jeannie and Lynn), Programs at the Reynolds
Homestead, Turner, Lynn and Marvin Foddrell playing music, Cap
Ayers making music, Lady Louise Clark, Ivan Weddle and Rufus Wood
making music, George Wood, Fair and displays at various events such as
the Vesta Fourth of July Celebration, Group photo (James Love, Mitty
McCarthy, Lucille Garrett, Daisy Pendelton, Linda Hopkins, Joanne
Alexander, Anita Cox, Joan Pfeifer, Leslie Shelor), Multiple photos of
moonshiners and Patrick County Project Van Stops in 1981.

Box 19
Grant proposals to National Endowment for the Humanities.
Final narrative report to NEH dated February 28, 1983.
Publicity materials such as newspaper clippings.

Box 20
Patrick County General Materials including photos, biographical sheets
that include genealogy, releases, field notes and tape logs for each
interview.

Box 22 Files with the following topics: Administration, Budget, Costs, Advisory Committee, Bibliography, Bibliography Orders, Complimentary Bibliography, Chairman Supplemental Grant, Film, Film Brochure, Correspondence, Evaluation, Financial Records, Impact Posters, Interim Narratives Reports, General.

Box 23 Correspondence

Box 24 Files with the following topics: NEH Quarterly Report, Recipes, Questionnaires (program, history alive, folk life program, community life, impact series, making a living), Summer Folk life Series, Summer Folk life Series Final Report, Releases, NEH Final Report, Public Programs (October 2 1980, Victorian Christmas, 1980-81, Winter-Spring 80-81, evaluation, Patrick County Fair, East Tennessee State University, Miscellaneous, crafts, historical society, Appalachian Book and Record Shop, Virginia Library Association), Film (correspondence, script, distribution, credit debate, brochure), Filming Meadows of Dan releases, Enterprise Indexing, Impact Series, Folklore (films, books, conference, Gooseberry Vine), Film Evaluation (Stuart, Meadows of Dan, Homestead), Film Correspondence, Impact Series (future programs, public programs, programs), Film-Edgerton brochure, Interview Subjects (correspondence, fair), Impact Series (scripts, conclusions, correspondence, Hard Times, Making a Living, Growing Up in Patrick County, Community Life), Content Analysis, Interviewers-Notes, Tapes and Transcripts.

Box 25 Files with the following topics: Press Clippings, Public Information, Press Releases, Promotional Materials, Public Program and Press Conference on October 2 1980, Publicity Correspondence, Press Kit, Memoranda, Library Orders, Library Materials, Mailing List, Advisory Committee Minutes, Mountain Passages, NEH Reports, Personnel, Memorandum of Understanding, Pictures of NEH Visit (Martin Sullivan), Posters, Printouts, Public Programs General, Reference Materials, Reynolds Homestead, PCP Summer 1980, Summer Folk life Series, Staff Meeting Minutes, Staff Meetings of February 13 1981, Staff Meeting of October 2 1981.

Box 26 Miscellaneous Papers
Box 27 Materials relating to the Citizens Committee For Public Libraries.

USING MATERIALS AT THE BLUE RIDGE REGIONAL LIBRARY

The Patrick County Branch of the Blue Ridge Regional Library contains cassette copies of all the interviews along with two copies of the six volume transcriptions.

Link to Patrick County Branch of the Blue Ridge Regional Library
http://www.brrl.lib.va.us/location_patrick.html
Link to Library Catalog of Blue Ridge Regional Library
http://www.brrl.lib.va.us/catalog.htm

Contact Information
116 W. Blue Ridge Street
P.O. Box 787
Stuart, Virginia 24171-0787
Phone:(276) 694-3352
Fax:(276) 694-6744
E-mail: patcolib@yahoo.com
Hours:
10 AM - 6 PM Monday & Wednesday
10 AM - 8 PM Tuesday & Thursday
10 AM - 2 PM Friday & Saturday

A Cassette player is available at the Patrick County Branch for patrons wishing to listen to the tapes.

Printed Materials from the catalog of the Blue Ridge Regional Library.

The Appalachian region of Virginia: a guide to library materials / compiled by Dorothy F. McCombs. Title (1981)
Locations: Patrick Reference VA
R VA COLL 016.9755 M
Bassett Reference R 016 M
Historical Center Reference R VA COLL 016.9755

A guide to materials for the Patrick County Project in the University Libraries: a select list of library materials on subjects of interest to the Project, either specific to Patrick County, or other appropriate titles from

the literature of local or regional studies. Compiled by Dorothy McCombs. Title (1981)
Locations: Patrick Adult Non-Fiction 016.9755
Patrick Reference VA Coll. R VA COLL 016.9755 M
Historical Center Reference Virginia R VA COLL 016.9755M

Patrick County: continuity and change in a rural community, a proposal submitted to the Library Humanities Program, Division of Public Programs, National Endowment for the Humanities, by the Blue Ridge Regional Library and Virginia Polytechnic Institute and State University. (1980)

Location: Patrick Reference R 975.569B
Patrick County: continuity and change in a rural community: oral history transcripts Patrick County Project. Title (1982)
Locations: Historical Center Reference Virginia R VA COLL 975.569 P

The Patrick County Project Oral History Collection: in the Special Collections Division, University Libraries, Virginia Polytechnic Institute and State University: a guide compiled by Dorothy McCombs. Title (1983)
Locations: Martinsville Reference VA Coll. R VA COLL 975.569 P
Patrick Reference R 975.569P
Historical Center Reference Virginia R VA COLL 975.569 P

INTERVIEWS

Interviews include interview subject, number of tapes, number of tapes transcribed, interviewer, date of interview and occupation of interview subject.

Ayers, Cary Goode 1 1 of 1 David Britt 18-May-81 Farmer/Basketweaver
Barbour, Andrew Lee Jr. 2 Excerpts from 1 John Reynolds 06-Dec-80 Saw Miller
Barnard Judy Lynn 1 1 of 1 Leslie Shelor 21-Apr-81 Equestrian
Barnard William 3 0 Joanne Alexander 04-Apr-81 Farmer/Contractor
Boaz, James Clayton 1 0 Daisy Pendleton 07-Dec-80 Newspaper publisher
Bolt, Ruth Jean and Lawrence 3 1 Side 1 of 2 Leslie Shelor 10-Jan, 8-Feb, 17-June-81 Teacher and her father
Carter, W. Curtis 2 0 John Reynolds 14-Jan-81 Lumber
Clark, Joseph Myron 4 0 David Britt 02-Apr-81 Merchant
Clark, Lady Louise 1 0 Mary Britt 05-Dec-80 Teacher/Librarian
Clark, Martin Filmore 1 1 of 1 Leslie Shelor 04-Feb-80 Attorney
Clark, Moir Ayers "Pete" 3 1, 2, 3 Joanne Alexander 28-Apr-81 Bus Driver/Teacher
Clark, Robert L. 2 1 Leslie Shelor 10-Dec-80 Merchant/Politicians
Clark, Ross 2 0 Walter Clark 14-Jun-81 Farmer
Clifton, Elder Bennie Neil 1 1 Walter Clark 27-Jan-81 Farmer/Carpenter
Clifton, Fred 1 1 Thompson and Shifflett 04-Nov-80 Teacher/Merchant
Cox, William Odell Sr. 2 0 John Reynolds 08-Dec-81 Park Ranger/Merchant
Cruise, Crystal Mae 2 Side 1 of 1 Lynn Terry 27-Jan-81 Teacher
Culler Caroline Bondurant 1 0 Leslie Shelor 11-Feb-82 Housewife
East, Gladys Fulcher 2 0 Doris Brown 01-Mar-82
Edwards, Sharon Allen 1 0 Daisy Pendleton 08-Dec-80 Farmer
Fain, Annie Lee Conner 1 0 Joanne L. Thomas 11-Jun-81 Housewife
Fain, Curtis Robert 1 1 Joanne L. Thomas 11-Jun-81 Orchard/lumber/construction
Foddrell, Marvin and Turner 4 1, 2, 3, 4 Donelion and Shifflett 21-Apr-81 Westinghouse/merchant
Foddrell, Posey Lester 1 1 Walter Clark 09-Apr-91 Farmer
Foley, Robert Earl 1 1 Joan Pfeifer Jul-81 Self-employed
Fulcher, Alice West 1 Excerpts of 1 Mitty McCarthy Jan-81 Housewife/textile worker

Fulcher, Albert "Rush" and Edith 2 0 Joan Pfeifer 04-Apr-81
Furniture/Textile/Fruit packer
Grady, Lucy Esther Vernon and Frank Banner 1 0 Doris Brown Mother
and Son
Hall, Dennis Howard 1 1 Joanne Thomas 31 and 7-June-1981
Farmer/Highway worker
Hall, Pearl Lillian 1 1 Walter Clark 16-Jun-81 Nurse
Handy, John P. and Novella S. 3 0 Arlene Keith 14-Nov-80 J. P. Stevens
Handy, Lilla Shelor 2 0 Leslie Shelor 01-Apr-82
Harbour, Kenneth Green 1 0 Daisy Pendleton 22-Nov-80 J. P. Stevens
Hardin Reynolds Elementary School 1 0 Joan Pfeifer 02-Apr-81 6th and
7th graders
Harris Hallie Pace 1 0 Doris Brown 01-Mar-82 Former Nurse
Harris, Lois Barnard 3 2 tapes Leslie Shelor 25-Apr-81 Retired Teacher
Harris, Oscar Allen 1 0 Daisy Pendleton 02-Dec-80
Minster/Retired/Contractor
Helms, Abrham and Eula Florence 1 0 Daisy Pendleton 08-Dec-80
Farmer and Housewife
Hooker, John Dillard 3 1, 2, 3 Lucille Garrett 13-Jan-81 Retired
Attorney/Judge
Hopkins, Earley Rufus and Beulah 7 Excerpts from 7 Anita Cox 01-Dec-
80 Merchant/MailCarrier/Farmer
Hopkins, Reverend Luther N. 1 Daisy Pendleton 13-Oct-80 Pastor
Hopkins, Walter Thomas Dudley 2 1, 2 Linda Hopkins 15-Nov-80
Retired Mail Carrier
Horton, Larry 3 0 Joanne Alexander 03-Feb-81 Highway Employee
Houchins, Mary Elizabeth Via 4 0 Joanne Alexander 01-Apr-81 Farmer
and Housewife
Howell, Ruby Underwood 1 Excerpts Leslie Shelor 2 thru 5-Nov-1980
Housewife
Hylton, Annie Hines 1 1 Phyllis Moore 03-Dec-80 Teacher
Hylton, Valentine Staples "Buddy" 1 1 James R. Plaster 22-Jun-81
Farmer and Merchant
Inscore, William Russell 2 0 Linda Hopkins 02-Dec-81
Farmer/Merchant/Driver
Jessup, Lula Emaline 4 0 Lynn Terry 10 and 24-Feb, 20-Mar-1983
Housewife
Kendrick, Jesse Enoch 1 0 Joan Pfeifer 16-Jan-81 Retired farmer,
sawmiller
Layman, William Edgar 1 1 Doris Brown 09-Jul-81 Plumber
McAlexander, Eunice 2 0 Leslie Shelor 18-Jun-83

McKenzie, Chester Nolan 7 0 Anita Cox 05-Jan-81 Cattle
Farmer/Housewife
Martin, Callie and Luther 1 0
Martin, Clarence McNeel 3 0 Reynolds and Brown 8-Jan, 3-Feb-1982
Retired farmer
Martin, Elizabeth Taliferro 1 0 Doris Brown 02-Feb-82 Teacher/cannery
manager
Mayo Mountain Singers 1 0
Mitchell, Ida Beasley 1 1 Linda Hopkins 30-Mar-81 Cannery/elastic
plant
Patrick County Cluster Event 1 0 Joanne Alexander May-81
Patrick County PEP Students *1 2 1, Side 1 of 2 Joan Pfeifer 25and26-
March-1981 4th Period Student
Pendleton, Buddy 2 1 Lynn Terry 24-Nov-80 World Fiddle Champion
Penn, Burgie Bett Lawson 1 1 Joan Pfeifer 13-Nov-80 Dietary
Supervisor
Pilson, Alpha Ella Morrison 2 Excerpts of 1 Anita Cox 03-Nov-80
Housewife
Pilson, Herbert G. 1 0 Walter Clark 13-Apr-81 Teacher/ mail carrier
Pilson, Ophus Eugene 4 0 Excerpts of 1 John Reynolds 04-Jun-81
Teacher and Principal
Plaster, James Russell 1 1 Joan Pfeifer 10-Feb-81 Retired Dupont
Engineer
Plaster, Lester Kyle 1 0 Davis Brown 01-Mar-83
Farmer/salesman/busdriver
Porter, Pamela Leigh 2 0 Joanne Alexander 31-Mar-81 Minister
Quilters Mary Horner Walker Church 1 0 Joanne Alexander 06-Jan-81
Lady quilters
Quilters of New Hope Church 1 0 Joanne Alexander 24-Feb-81 Lady
quilters
Rakes, Ovilla Sue 2 1 Daisy Pendleton 01-Oct-80 Teacher, quilter,
crafter
Roberson, Winifred Cox 1 1 Walter Clark 10-Jun-81 Teacher, Postal
worker
Shelor, Bertie Marshall 2 1,2 Leslie Shelor 25-Jan-81 Housewife
Shelor, James R. and Clay 2 0 Lynn Terry 24 and 31-March-1981
Banker
Shelor, Jesse and Clarice 4 3,4 Terry and Shiflett 31-Dec, 6-Jan-1981
Highway/Housewife
Shelor, William E. and Alice Belt 1 0 Lynn Terry 28-Jan-81 J. P.
Stevens/teacher

Slate, Robert Samuel and Sally T. Hill 5 All Joanne Alexander 11-Nov, 3&10-Dec-1980 Farmer/Saw Miller

Spangler, Charles Langhorne "Tump" 4 1,2,3,4 Mitty McCarthy 20-Mar-81 Farmer/State Employee

Spangler, Dorn Odell 2 1,2 Claudette Thompson 13-Nov-80 School Superintendent

Strock, Stella May Hodges 3 1,2,3 Joanne Alexander 17-Jan-81 Retired School Teacher

Stuart Elementary School Students 1 1, Joan Pfeifer 31-Mar-81 Sixth/Seventh Graders

Terry, Mary Sue 4 1,2,3 Joanne Alexander 20-Jul-81 Attorney

Terry, Nannie Ruth 3 T1S2,T2S1,T3S1 Mary Britt 07-Nov-80 Retired Teacher

Thomas, Josie G. 1 0 Joanne Thomas 31-Jul-81 Housewife

Thompson, Murray Edward 3 1,2,3 Joanne Alexander 30-Oct-80 Retired Teacher

Trinity Church of God 4 0 Joan Pfeifer 22-Feb-81 Church service

Turner, Edward M. 3 0 County Administrator

Turner, John J. and Gracey Wilson 3 0 John Reynolds 28-Apr-81 Farmer/textile/lumber

Weaver, Gertrude Wimbush 1 1 Walter Clark 30-Apr-81 Retired Teacher

Weaver, Walter Noel 1 1 Walter Clark 20-Feb, 20-March-1981 J. P. Stevens

Williams, Dudley Stanley 3 0 Joanne Alexander 02-Jun-81 Farmer

Williams, Lena Lampe (Mrs. Glen A.) 3 1,2,3 Joanne Alexander 18-Apr-81 Home-maker, widow

Williams, Virgil and Ella Lowell 1 0 Daisy Pendleton 06-Nov-80 Self-employed/Housewife

Williams, Woodrow 1 0 Lucille Garrett

Wood, Addie Jane 2 0 Mitty McCarthy 28-Jan, 5-Feb-1981 Farmer

Wood, Eunice Moore 1 1 Doris Brown 19-Jun-81 Retired Teacher

Wood, George Edgar "Bill" 3 0 Doris Brown 19-Feb-82 Retired Mail Carrier

Wood, George Stephen and Claudia 2 1 Mitty McCarthy 31-Oct-80 Farmer/Teacher

Wood, Robert Amos 1 0 Walter Clark 13-Apr-81 Farmer

Woodall, Ethel 1 0 Phyllis Moore 01-Nov-80 Storeowner

Woolwine Elementary School 2 0

Worley, Lucy Thomas 1 Excerpts of 1 Daisy Pendleton 19-Dec-80 Retired School Teacher

ABSTRACTS

Interview, Subject and Topics Covered

Ayers, Basketmaking
Barbour, Sawmilling, Primitive Baptist Church meetings, entertainment before radio and television, wheat threshings, cornshuckings and midwives
Barnard J., Returning to Patrick County after living in city and concerns over young people
Barnard W., Kibler Valley, pioneers, land grants, indians, courtdays, churches, cemeteries, parks, Dinky Railroad, brandy, diving rods
Boaz, History of The Enterprise newspaper, changes brought by roads and radios,
Bolt, Farm life, women's life, schools, history of county, roads and parks, Blue Ridge Parkway
Carter, Danville and Western Railroad
Clark, J., Clark Brothers Store, merchandise, supplies by wagon and railroad, customers, The Depression, Christmas visits, dances, circus, hotels
Clark, L., Stuart Public Library, Stuart's Woman's Club, Patrick County Historical Society
Clark, M.F., Politics, law, government, jails, finance, juveniles, school system, property and family responsibilities
Clark, M.A., Farm life, schools, roads, The Depression, loss of train
Clark, R., Farming, self-sufficiency, dairies, orchards, county agents, open range, doctors, hospitals, power and water systems, lumber, railroads
Clark, Ross, Farming, Tobacco, music and socializing, beekeeping, blacksmithing, butchering
Clifton, E., Country stores, Chestnut trees, shipping routes for produce, peddlers, high elevation pastures, "sheep shelter caves", tanning bark
Clifton, Fred, Teaching, College at William and Mary, clearing land, buckwheat, honey, sawmills, changes brought by roads
Cox, Civilian Conservation Corps at Fairy Stone Park, Park Ranger, Tobacco, Orchards, bartering
Cruise, Schools, Teaching, quilts, home remedies, hospital volunteer work
Culler, The Hollow, home-made clothing, roads, tobacco farming
East, Boarding houses, Danville and Western Railroad, hospital, home remedies

Edwards, Farm life, hunting, soap making, chestnuts, Blue Ridge Parkway, life before radios and cars

Fain, A., Rye Cove, Dobyns, changes in homemaking, folklore, home remedies, bartering, rural mail carrier, post offices, singing schools˙

Fain, C., Brushy Fork area, schools, Primitive Baptist Associations, court days, scary tales, The Depression, chestnuts, tanning, hospitals, doctors

Foddrell, M. T., Five Forks, Country and Blues music (Brothers)

Foddrell, P., Growing up an orphan, sharecropping, Clark family, veterinary work, well digging, tobacco, music

Foley, Farm life, schools, roads, race car driving

Fulcher, Alice, Childhood, schools, chores such as plucking feathers off ducks, food preservation, home remedies and funerals

Fulcher, Albert, Making molasses and apple butter, soap and washing clothes, corn shucking, tobacco curing, wheat threshing, gypsies, peddlers, quilting

Grady, Schools in Nettle Ridge, roads, hunting, crops, mills and county stores

Hall, D., Farming food and preserving it, bartering, country stores, chestnuts, butter, eggs, hunting wildcats, ghosts, midwives, home remedies

Hall, P., Childhood in Goblintown area, milling, furniture, coffin making, raising cotton, flax, spinning clothing, Fayerdale, Ferrum College

Handy, J., Funerals, children, sports, baseball, butter making, radio, cars, tobacco farming, preserving food

Handy, L., Farming with oxen, country stores, darning socks, building roads, epidemics, home remedies, casket making, children's games and toys

Harbour, Depression, blacksmiths, sawmills, J. P. Stevens, roads, car races, antique cars

HRES, Life in Patrick County, chores, jobs.

Harris, H., Stuart Hospital, nursing

Harris, L., Raising flax and sheep, spinning, weaving and making clothes, log houses, newspapers, reading, college education, World Wars, schools

Harris, O., Changes in churches, spending Sundays, carpentry, first car and radio, chestnuts

Helms, A., Rural living, games, dances, courting, roads, bootlegging, J. P. Stevens, first car and radio

Hooker, Depression, CWA, WPA, government, schools, court, attorneys, jail, rock quarry, rock in building roads

Hopkins, E., Apple Orchards, country stores, Central Academy, roads
built by convicts, making shoes, fairs, reunions, Yankee plunder, dances

Hopkins, R., Leaving and returning to county, Smith River Church of the
Brethren

Hopkins, W., Buffalo Ridge, country stores, large families, trundle beds,
holidays, tan bark, lighting homes by carbide, fairystones, bootlegging,
road

Horton, Log Cabins, fireplaces, traditional tools, schools, fishing, Kibler
Valley

Houchins, Childhood and parents who were slaves, church, Bible,
integration, child-rearing, home remedies, Fairystone Park

Howell, Rock Castle Gorge, family, weddings, shearing sheep, carding,
spinning, War Between the States, singing and boarding school, women

Hylton A., Childhood, one room schools, bus accidents, cutting pulp
wood for college tuition, schools for blacks, integration, religious faith

Hylton, V., Buying and selling blackberries to food company, neighbors,
changes in family and community life

Inscore, Moonshining, grocery store owner

Jessup ,Family photo album, clothing, spinning, weaving, suits,
coverlets, blankets, snuff, teeth, dentists, school breakings, spelling bees

Kendrick, Mills and grinding corn, making molasses and soap, hunting,
fishing, CCC camps, guitars and music, butchering, cars

Layman, Drying apples and blackberries, community stores, livery
stables, brick making, railroad, electricity

McAlexander, Folk music, Cecil Sharp, Dr. Arthur Kyle-Davis, farming,
clothing, woolen mill on Burke's Fork, soap, chestnuts, molasses,
weddings

McKenzie, Sycamore Baptist Church, Blue Ridge Mission School,
World War Two, modern farming, education, children's lives

Martin, Callie

Martin, Clarence, Work on railroads, furniture and textile mills, church,
social life, D & W Railroad, gristmills, cornmeal

Martin, Elizabeth, Critz, schools, candy factory, blackberry cannery,
Cooper's Mill, Delco plant, sidewalks, railroads, father's store

Mayo Mountain, Mitchell Church activities, ghost stories, barn raisings,
early marriage and large families, The Depression

PCCE, PCHS Allowances, drug problems, employment opportunities,
recreation, discipline, future of county, religion, music, tourism

Pendleton, Fiddling with bands and competitions, instruments, music for
good and bad purposes

Penn, Church and music, mother as minister, weddings, funerals, youth and family reunions

Pilson A., Family, early marriage, raising eight children, church

Pilson, H., Changes in county, roads, electricity, movement from mountains to piedmont, newcomers from urban area

Pilson, O., Schools, discipline, compulsory attendance, sports, growing up in Patrick County, farming, hunting, local history, tombstone inscriptions

Plaster, J., Patrick Spring Resort, train wrecks, gold mines, No Business Mountain, Changes in county, electricity, roads, World War Two

Plaster, L., Driving trucks, school bus, first car in county, roads, electricity, telephones, orchards, The Depression, chestnuts, WPA, World War Two

Porter, Ministry, parent's support, education, study in France, Fellowship Church

Quilter MHWC, Quilting

Quilters NHC, Quilting

Rakes, Nolin, Rakes families, widowed mother raising children, country store, ice cream sales, murder of bootlegger informant, epidemics,

Roberson, Churches, schools, widowed mother raising children, root washing service and mission schools

Shelor B., Farm life, schooling in the early 1900s, spinning, weaving, homegrown flax, wool, World War Two, newcomers, Parkway

Shelor, James, Play, games, pranks, school, family reunions, music, church, changes in the county

Shelor, Jesse, Traditional mountain music, typhoid fever, blacksmithing, road work

Shelor, William, Roads for mountain areas, Blue Ridge Parkway, music, family at singing schools, dances, church, fiddle playing, flat-footing, clogging

Slate, Families in early 1900s, clearing land, corn, tobacco, butchering, horsetrading, food preservation

Spangler C., Land grants, Indians, Early settlers, Langhornes, chestnuts, box factory, Black cemetery, Mayberry, revenue officer, Allen tragedy

Spangler, D., Schools consolidation, discipline, The Depression, industry, World War Two, sickness, unemployment, funerals, marriage

Strock, Teaching in public and church schools, Radford College, clothing, toys, weddings, women's lives

SES, Living in Patrick County, chores, sports, stores, industry, jobs, television, use of land, newcomers

Terry, M.S., Early life in Patrick County, parents, school experiences, law career, politics, changes in county, women's rights, integration

Terry, N.R., School funding, boarding, consolidation, integration, Cooper's Mill, pig farming, electricity, horse-back riding, World's Fair

Thomas, Food preservation, hominy, cloth making, weaving, spinning, chestnuts, midwives, doctors, epidemics, hospitals, funerals

Thompson, Children's toys, chores, holidays, square dancing, livery stables, newspapers, prohibition, furniture, caskets, barbers, "individualism"

Trinity, Evangelist Alice Hairston, singing and music

Turner, E., Agriculture, flood of 1979, fire rescue squads, vocational education, church's role in community, welfare, local government, recreation

Turner, J., Indians, Fort Mayo, Iron works at Fayerdale, photos of historic sites in Patrick, factory work versus farming

Weaver, G., Jeb Stuart Statue, hotels, restaurants, livery stable, church activities, schools and teaching

Weaver, W., Milling, carpentry, caskets bootlegging, chestnuts, dried apples, wild hogs, Church, singing, square dancing, corn shucking, quilting

Williams, D., Music, dancing, playing making banjos, guitars, flat-footing, square dancing, distillery, apple brandy, herbs, home remedies, "French man"

Williams, L., Husband was minister of Presbyterian churches and mission schools at Blue Ridge, quilting, rag rugs, Kibler Valley

Williams, V., Lumber industry, sawmilling, changes in women's lifestyle, roads

Williams, W., Large families, making and washing clothes, picking duck for pillows, bed ticks, Christmas, pet bear, moonshining

Wood, A., Family farm life, drying foods, soap making, tanning, epidemics 1913 1919, nursing, burial, coffins, boarding students, mission schools

Wood, E., Teaching, retirement

Wood, George E., Patrick Spring Resort, fox hunting, woman's college, mail carrying, packing apples, No Business Mountain, bootlegging, saloons

Wood, George S., Growing up on farms, homemade shoes, homemade clothing, bartering chestnuts, corn shucking, log rolling, apple butter, reunions

Wood, R., Farming with oxen, building stone houses, hunting and guns

Woodall. Prices and Store Customers

Change comes slow to Patrick County reflected in the original Patrick County Courthouse in the town formerly known as Taylorsville, now Stuart, Virginia.

NAME AND SUBJECT INDEX
Name or Subject, Interview Subject, Tape, Side, Counter Reading

Abbington, Bill Houchins, L 3 1 89
Adams, Bill Spangle, R C 3 1 176, 194
Adams, Notley "Not" Weaver, N 1 2 590
Affluence Harris, O 1 1 224
Kendrick, J 1 2 232
Penn, B 1 2 232
Agee, Leonard Shelor, J R 2 2 367
Aging Barnard, J 1 1 219
Clark, J M 3 1 200
Houchins, M 4 2 72
Strock, 3 2 234-380
Williams, L 2 2 234
Stuart E S 1 2 25
Angle, Mrs. Turner, J J 3 1 150
Airplanes Barnard, W 3 2 227, 237
Spangler, D O 2 2 404
Turner, J J 3 2 513, 545
Akers, Charles A Hopkins E & B 1 1 194 2 2 25
Akers, Mrs. C.A. McKenzie, C & E 2 1 94
Akers, Dade McKenzie, C & E 2 2 25
Akers, Dewey Thompson, M E 1 2 117
Akers, Ike Hopkins, E & B 1 1 94 2 2 25
Akers, (Dr.) W.C. Clark, M A 2 2 134
Harris, H P 1 1 74, 122
Martin, C M 2 2 550
Wood, G E 1 1 380 2
Akers, Dr. Walter Curtis Harris, H 1 1 115, 136, 226, 298
1 2 525, 540, 701, 763
Alcohol Porter, P 2 2 126
Allen, Claude Spangler, C 3 2 165, 199, 35
Allen, Daniel Bolt, R J 1 2 352
Allen, Floyd Spangler, C 3 2 165,199,277,309,328
Allen, Nancy (wife of Nathan W) Hopkins, E & B 3 1 119
Allen, Nathan Hopkins, E & B 3 1 119
Allen Tragedy- Carroll County Spangler, C 3 2 154, 165, 183, 199,
Courthouse Tragedy 222, 278, 309, 328
Wood, G & C 2 2 400, 450
Wood, A 1 2 158

Clifton, F 1 1 210, 317
Allowances Patrick County HS 2 1 68
Animals Bolt, R 3 1 226,330
William, W 1 1 20
Wood, A S 1 1 111, 125, 136
Antiques Martin, E 1 2 854
Anthony, Arthur Terry, N R 3 2 92
Anthony, Charles Carter, W C 2 1 165
Anthony, Clarence Carter, W C 2 1 165
Appendicitis Jessup, L 1 1 185
Apple Orchards
Williams, D 2 1 437 2 2 30
Wood, C E 1 2 553
Martin, C M 3 1 189 250
Slate, R & S 4 2 285
Martin, C M 2 1 383
Hall, D 1 1 216
Hopkins, B & E 1 1 161
Weaver, N 1 1 289 3
Ararat Inscore, W R 2 2 166
Ardner, Bob Carter, W C 1 1 269
Arrington, Bob Thomas, J 1 1 378
Arts, Crafts Rakes, O 1 1 115
Ashby, W.L. Clark, R L 1 2 264
Weaver, G 1 1 537
Ashby, Walter Martin, C M 1 1 190
Assassination Stuart E S 1 2 100, 130
Atkins, Joe McKenzie, C & E 1 1 125
Atkins, Will McKenzie, C & E 1 1 125
Attorney, Law Practice Thompson, M E 2 2 177
Automobiles Boaz, J 1 1 33 1 1 275
Bolt, R 1 2 436 2 1 20
Clark, M A 1 1 213, 265 1 2 362 2 1 246
Clifton, F 1 2 243
Culler, C 1 1 70, 107
Edwards, M 1 1 250
Foley, R 1 1 264
Handy, J & N 2 2 212
Hall, P 1 2 123, 143
Harris, L 1 1 408
Helms, A & E 1 1 248, 750

Hopkins, B & E 2 1 56
Hopkins, L 1 1 217
Horton, L 2 1 208
Inscore, F R 1 1 248 2 2 74
Kendrick, J 1 2 270, 422
Martin, C M 1 1 100
Pilson, A 1 1 357
Shelor, B 2 2 369
Slate, R & S 1 1 168 2 1 220
Spangler, C 4 2 240, 252, 308
Spangler, D O 2 2 380, 404 4
Thomas, J 1 1 168 1 2 254
Turner, J J 3 2 580
Racing, History, Antique Williams, D 2 1 34, 269
Williams, W 1 1 250 1 2 460, 680
Wood, G & C 1 2 50, 100
Wood, G E 3 1 66 3 1 228
Worley, L 1 2 496
Plaster, L 1 2 635
Harbour, K 1 2 457
Barnard, W 1 2 49, 58
Clifton, B 1 2 38
Racing, History, Antique Harris, O 1 1 203
Hopkins, W 1 2 290
Wood, R M 1 2 781
Hylton, B 1 1 354
Cox, W 2 2 472
Foley, R 1 2 177-267
Clark, M F 2 2 152, 165
Thompson, M E 1 2 81, 47 2 1 223, 232, 305, 336 2 2 319, 330
Averett College McKenzie, C & E 1 1 162
Ayers, Christine Critz Terry, N R 1 2 404
Martin, E T 1 2 724
Ayers, Linwood Martin, E T 1 2 724
Ayers School Thompson, M E 1 1 179
Balilles, (Jerry) Gerald Pilson, O E 3 2 507
Clark, L 1 2 132
Baliles, Lee Pilson, O E 3 2 472
Baliles, Posey L Pilson, O E 3 2 507
Banks, Banking Layman, W 1 2 763
Wood, R A 1 2 119

Banks, Tilden Jessup, 2 1 27
Baptism Thompson, M R 3 1 139
Houchins, M 1 1 300 5 3 1 365
Jessup, L 2 1 311, 360
Barbers Thompson, M E 2 2 350
Barbour, Jim Pete Barber, A L 1 1 58, 130
Barker, Red Pendleton, B 1 1 273
Barksdale, Capt. Carter, W C 1 1 269
Barksdale, Mabel Weaver, G 1 1 35
Barn Raisings Boaz, J 1 1 22
Hylton, B 1 1 203
Mitchell, I 1 1 153
Slate, R & S 4 2 99
Barnard, Alice Clifton, F 1 1 110
Jessup, 1 2 151
Barnard, Alvin Harris, L B 1 1 128 2 1 87
Barnard, Archie Barnard, W 1 1 44
Barnard, Daniel Jessup, 1 1 125 4 2 28
Barnard, Elijah Thomas, J 1 1 378
Barnard, Elisha Thomas, J 1 1 378
Barnard, Ida Jessup, 1 2 182
Barnard, Isom Barnard, W 1 1 48, 52, 336
Barnard, Jeff Jessup, 1 2 56 3 2 224
Barnard, Jehu Harris, L 1 1 128 2 1 87
Barnard, Johnny Jessup, 4 2 133
Barnard, Judy Lynn Barnard, J L 1
Barnard, Letha Jessup, 4 2 56 6 3 2 224
Barnard, Levi Spangler, C 4 2 105
Barnard, Louise Jessup, 1 1 125
Barnard, William Barnard, W 1,2,3
Horton, 2 1 39
Barnes, Ison Barnard, W 2 2 307
Bartering Bolt, R 1 2 304
Hall, D 1 1 132, 172
Handy, J & N 1 1 20
Hopkins, B & E 1 1 123
Hopkins, W 1 1 325
Layman, W 1 1 173
McKenzie, C & E 5 1 427 5 2 24
Martin, C M 2 1 285
Martin, L & C 1 1 323

Shelor, B 1 1 109
Baseball Handy, J & N 1 1 125-308 1 2 213 2 1 187-410
Pilson, O E 2 2 3(840)
Basketball Clark, M A 1 2 180
Terry, N R 2 1 286
Hopkins, R & R 5 2 441 6 1 26
Basket Making Ayers, C 1 1 1 2
Bassett Chair Factory (Furniture) Kendrick, J 1 2 136
Cox, W 1 1 35, 70
Bateman, Harriet Hall, D 1 1 97
Baths Martin, 3 2 507
Brady, F & L 1 1 321
Williams, W 1 2 199
Battle, Governor John Hooker, J 3 1 132 7
Beans Martin, C M 3 1 357, 368, 397, 415
Beaseley, Marshall Carter, W C 2 2 650
Beds Martin, L & C 1 1 300
Fulcher, A W 1 2 139
Inscore, W R 1 2 173, 209
Williams, D 2 2 144
Wood, A 2 2 180, 195, 212
Wood, C & L 1 2 300
Wood, G E 2 1 359, 407, 470
Bee Hives Williams, D 3 2 121
Bee Keeping Clark, R 1 2 270
Beef Martin, C M 2 2 690
Belton, Hamilton (Ham) Foddrell, P 1 1
Belton's Store Foddrell, P 1 1 30
Bell Spur Church Harris, L 1 2 403
Berries Martin, L & C 1 2 536, 559, 564
Berries Plaster, L 1 1 284
Handy, J & N 2 2 94
Bethel Baptist Church McKenzie, C & E
Beverly, Barbara Jessup, 2 1 185
Beverly, Bill Clifton, F 1 1 149
Beverly, Lizzie (Lynch) Jessup, 1 1 107
Bible Reading, School Houchins, M 2 2 169
Williams, L 2 1 343
Big A School Clark, R L 1 1 175
Biggs, G.P. Fulcher, R & E 1 2 167
Biggs, Tod Spangler, C 4 1 250

Bishop, Francis Wood, G E 1 2 485 8
Bishop, John Fulcher, A 1 2 287
Blackard, Martin, C M 1 1 190
Blackard, Edgar Thomas, J 1 1 198
Blackard, Ernest Thomas, J 1 1 198
Blackard, Julian Cruise, C 1 2 117
Blackard, Lillie or Lilly Bolt, 1 2 54
Blackard, W.G. Hooker, J 2 1 275
Blackard, Wilbur Clifton, F 1 1 46
Blackjack School Hylton, A H 1 2 62, 70
Blacks, Discrimination Clark, J M 1 2 158
Churches Clifton, B 1 1 77
Hall, P 1 2 319
Slate, R & S 2 1 231
Spangler, C 1 2 428 3 1 120, 194, 241
Terry, M S 2 2 88
Thompson, M E 2 2 363
Williams, L 1 2 221
Terry, N R 2 2 401
Carter, 1 2 623
Hylton, A H 1 1 300, 377, 440
Blacks 1 2 1, 82, 165
Trinity Church of God 1-4
McKenzie, C & E 2 1 295, 313
Barbour, 1 1 329, 430
Houchins, 1 1 133
Clifton, F 1 1 67
Blacksmiths Clark, R 1 2 270
Hall, D 1 2 437
Layman, W 1 1 287
Martin, C M 3 2 726
Shelor, J & C 4 1 315
Harbour, K 1 1 265
Blindness Spangler, C 1 1 178, 218 2 1 59, 105
Blue Ridge Baptist Association McKenzie, C & E 2 1 75 9
Blue Ridge Candy Company Martin, K 1 1 164, 276
Blue Ridge Elementary School Porter, P 2 2 315
Blue Ridge Institute Clifton, F 1 1 20
Blue Ridge Mission School Pilson, O E 1 1 380 1 2 576
Roberson, W 1 1 30
McKenzie, C & E 2 1 95 3 1 27, 174, 226, 262 3 2 93 4 1 246 5 2 150

Blue Ridge Parkway Bolt, R 1 1 188 2 1 162
Edwards, M 1 1 316
Fain, C 1 2 11
Helms, A & E 1 2 232
Howell, R 1 1 175
Jessup, L 4 2 3
Shelor, R 2 2 316
Shelor, W & A 1 2 135, 168
Wood, G & C 2 2 200, 250
Worley, L 1 2 631
Clifton, F 1 1 329
Boarding Houses East, G 1 1 45, 57 2 2 543
Weaver, G 1 1 540
Bolt, S L Shelor, W & A 1 1 154
"Boogur Light" Bolt, R 1 1 57
Books, Reading Shelor, B 2 1 24
Boone, Ben East, G 2 1 238
Boone, Flora East, G 2 1 62
Bottling Co, Soft Drinks Layman, W 1 1 115-190
Bouldin Memorial Presbyterian Hopkins, B & E 3 1 78
Church 4 2 112, 211 10
Bowman, Andrew Barnard, W 3 1
Bowman, Caroline Jessup, 3 2 110
Bowman, Coolidge Horton, 1 1 88
Bowman, Cora Jessup, 1 1 185 1 2 94
Bowman, Delbert Jessup, 3 1 140
Bowman, Flora Jessup, 4 1 82
Bowman, George Jessup, 4 1 196
Bowman, Gloria Walker, M H 1 1 39
Bowman, Helen Shelor, J R 1 2 31
Bowman, Jess Jessup, 3 1 140
Bowman, Ona Pilson, A 1 2 137
Bowman, Preston Jessup, 3 1
Box Functions Spangler, C 2 2 241, 298, 332
Boyce, William Wood, G E 1 2 669
Boyd, John Carter, W C 1 1 269
Boyd, Sam Harris, L B 1 1 173
Brammer, Noel Thompson, 1 1 248
Brammer School Turner, J J 3 1 175
Brandy Barnard, W 1 1 402, 433
Bread Baking Slate, R & S 1 1 40

Bream, Sara Spangler, C 3 2 382
Brick Laying Slate, R & S 1 2 23, 116
Layman, W 1 2 531-546
Brim, Ethel Hylton, A 1 1 420 11
Brown, John Terry, N R 2 2 211
Brown, Pearl Terry, M S 1 2 107
Brown School Terry, N R 1 2 184
Bruce, David K. (Ambassador) Clark, L L 1 1 33
Brushy Fork Fain, C 1 1 33
Bryant, Alec Pilson, A 2 1 62
Bryant, Alexander McKenzie, 2 1 65
Bryant, Tom Clifton, F 1 2 41
Buck Dancing Foddrell, M & T 1 2 101 3 2 202
Buckwheat Clifton, F 1 1 184
Buckwheat Cakes Fulcher, A W 1 1 345
Buffalo Ridge Pentecostal McKenzie, C & K 2 1 239
Holiness Church Pilson, A 1 2 89-137 2 1 135
Buggies Pilson, A 1 1 432
Bullins, Dee Foddrel, M & T 2 1 42
Burch, Belle McKenzie, M 3 1 68
Burgart, Joe Wood, G E 1 1 245
Burgart, Mr. East, G 2 1 24
Burgart, Mrs. Dora Wood, G E 1 1 245
Burgart's Store Layman, W 1 3 524
Burge, Walter Slate, 4 2 312
Burnett, Matt Bolt, 3 2 95
Shelor, J R 2 2 214
Burnette, Jim Jessup, 1 1 25
Burnette, Lee Jessup, 1 1 25 12
Burton, Alice Hopkins, E B 4 2 401
Burton, Frank Sr. Thompson, 3 1 61
Clark, L 1 1 33
Clark, M F 1 2 253 3 1 51
Buses, Busing Clark, M A 1 1 273
Clark, R L 1 1 50
Fulcher, R & E 2 1 249
Slate, R & S 3 1 362
Hylton, A H 1 1 355
Plaster, L 1 1 64
Thompson, M 1 2 137
Pilson, O 2 1 414

Plaster, L 1 2 577, 598, 705
Shelor, J R 1 1 125
Businesses Clark, M A 2 1 34
Williams, V 1 2 668
Busted Rock Edwards, M 1 1 159
Clifton, B 1 1 115
Buggies, Surries Boaz, J 1 1 33
East, A 1 1 171, 204
Buzz Wagons Hooker, J 1 1 149
Thompson, M E 1 2 130
"Byrd Machine" Hooker, J 3 1 95
Cabbage Clifton, B 1 1 371
Callahan Shelor, J R 2 1 234
Callaway, Ruffin "Ruff" Jessup, 1 1 319
Campgrounds, Camping Hopkins, R & E 2 1 116 2 2 335
Barbour, A 1 2 533, 676 2 1 268
Canals Spangler, C 1 2 358, 382
Cancer Harris, H 1 1 462, 496, 500 13
Cannady, Jenny Hall, P 1 1 319
Canneries Martin, E 1 1 340-389
Slate, R & S 2 1 160
Carnivals Shelor, J R 2 2 10
Carpentry Ayers, C 1 1 69
Weaver, N 1 1 50
Carroll Turnpike Hopkins, R & E 1 2 101
(Witt Spur, Trot Valley Road)
Carter Martin, C M 2 2 527
Carter, Crawford East, G 1 1 109
Carter, Cy Thompson, 2 1 99
Carter, Eldrin Turner, J J 1 2 660
Carter, Elma Clark, L 1 1 231
Carter, Jefferson T Carter, W C 1 1 35
Carter, Joe Spangler, C 3 1 215
Carter, Kibler Turner, J J 1 2 620
Carter, L.G. Spangler, C 1 1 90
Carter, Lloyd Layman, 1 2 650
Carter, Reed Martin, C M 3 1 229
Carter, Sly Martin, C M 2 1 690
Carter, Taft Turner, J J 1 2 660
Carter, Troy Turner, J J 1 2 620
Fulcher, R & E 1 1 128

Carter, W. C. Layman, 1 1 80
Carter, W. Curtis Carter, W C 1, 2
Carter's Chapel Porter, P 1 1 104, 147 14
Caskets Weaver, N 1 1 90, 75, 85, 100
Culler, C 1 2 226
Handy, L 1 1 143
Cassell, Dewey Clifton, E N 1 1 137
Cassidy, Willie Foddell, M & T 2 1 42
Cattle Handy, J & H 1 2 137
Grady, F & R 1 1 277, 291
Martin, C H 2 1 267
Cavender, Dick Houchins, 3 1 68
Cemeteries Barnard, W 2 2 385, 396, 420
Harris, L 2 1 105
Pilson, O 3 2 585, 442, 479
Censorship Clark, L L 1 1 294
Census Houchins, M 1 2 154
Central Academy Clifton, F 1 1 210
Cruise, C 1 1 204, 348
Spangler, D O 1 1 22
Strock, 1 2 22, 36, 87
Thomas, J 1 2 370
Williams, W 1 1 101
Hopkins, B & E 4 2 146 6 2 200 5 2 338
Chamber of Commerce Clark, M F 2 2 30, 40
Charity Rakes, A O 1 1 2, 21
Bootlegging Clark, M F 2 2 321
Clifton, F 1 2 41
Worley, L 1 1 22
Chemicals Wood, G E 1 1 606, 637
Cherries Martin, C M 3 2 625
Chestnut Barnard, W 3 2 162
Carter, W 1 1 436
Hall, D 1 2 132
Pilson, A 1 1 300
Rakes, O 1 2 140 15
Thomas, J 1 2 111
Wood, G & C 1 1 70, 220
Boaz, J 1 2 713
Edwards, M 1 1 324
Fain, C 1 2 238

Harris, O 1 2 630
Helms, A & E 1 2 196
Hopkins, W 1 1 340
Chestnut Hopkins, B & E 7 1 114
McKenzie, C & E 5 1 378
Slate, R & S 3 1 200
Spangler, C 1 2 106, 124, 138, 149, 150, 167
Thomas, J 1 2 154
Worley, L 1 2 603
Hopkins, B & E 1 1 218
Clifton, F 1 2 134
Plaster, L 1 1 135
Shelor, J & C 2 2 367-454
Weaver, N 1 1 289, 309
Chestnut Grove Church Porter, P 1 1 124
Chickens Wood, A 2 1 210, 245, 259
Shelor, B 1 1 122
Children, Rearing Culler, C 1 2 193
Childbirth Spangler, D O 1 2 274, 324
Childhood Culler, C 1 2 36
East, G 2 2 580
Harris, H 1 1 402
Hylton, B 1 1 338
Jessup, L 2 1 377, 418
Slate, R & S 2 1 355, 390 2 2 34
Weaver, N 1 1 35
Williams, D 2 1 185
Wood, A 1 2 142
Wood, G E 2 2 749
Martin, L & C 1 2 674
Fulcher, A W 1 1 308 1 2 260
Terry, M S 2 2 239
Childhood Games Handy, L 1 2 187, 228
Weaver, G 1 1 7, 35
Wood, G E 2 1 232
Boaz, J 1 2 453
Helms, A & E 1 2 250 16
Barnard, W 3 1 188, 202
Edwards, M 1 1 286
Harbour, K 1 2 709
Inscore, W R 1 1 216

Martin, L & C 1 1 340
Slate, R & S 2 1 268, 279 2 2 210
Thompson, M E 2 2 364, 394, 415 3 1 199
Williams, W 1 1 234, 249, 259
Wood, G & C 1 2 150
Howell, R 1 1 39
Clark, J M 4 1 89
Martin, C M 2 1 169, 185, 196, 214
Barnard, W 2 1 150, 160
Christmas Boaz, J 1 1 356,360
Cruise, L 1 1 120
East, G 1 1 301
Hall, P 1 2 116
Hopkins, B & E 3 1 78
Hopkins, L 1 1 141, 163
Martin, E 1 2 610
Rakes, O 1 2 19
Roberson, W 1 1 251
Shelor, B 2 1 195
Strock, 1 2 50, 78 2 2 135
Weaver, G 1 1 380, 430
William, L 1 1 53, 103 1 2 80 2 2 52 3 1 357
Wood, E M 1 2 570
Penn, B 1 1 296 1 1 103 1 2 1
Houchins, M 1 2 289
Trinity Church of God 1-4
Turner, E M 1 2 175
Harris, L 1 2 403
Church, Don Martin, C M 2 1 700
Plaster, L 1 1 92
Churches Houchins, M 1 1 335 18
Jessup, L 4 2 133
Hall, P 1 1 202
Turner, E M 1 2 136, 158, 175
Weaver, N 1 2 85
Williams, L 2 1 367
Clifton, B 1 1 250
Culler, C 1 1 213
Handy, L 1 2 324, 415
Helms, A & E 1 1 177 1 2 105
Mitchell, I 1 1 290 1 2 216

Clark, George (Dr.) Clark, R L 1 2 175
Clark, Hazel Young Clark, M F 1 1 260, 278, 290 2 2 118 3 1 44
Clark, Henry Clark, M F 1 1 172, 197
Clark, Jacob Clark, R L 1 2 331
Clark, Jane Stovall Clark, R L 1 2 331
Clark, J.J. Foddrell, P 1 1 215
Clark, John Thompson, 1 2 147
Clark, John R. Sr. Clark, R 1 2 110
Clark, Mabel T. (Mrs. Walter E.) Weaver, G 1 1 440
Clark, Mack Foddrell, P 1 1 400
Clark, "Mack" Clark, Ross 1 2 231 20
Clark, Martin F. ("Phil") Thompson 2 2 275
Martin, C M 2 2 750
Terry, M S 1 1 47
Clark, Marshall Foddrell, M & T 2 1 71
Clark, Mary Carlton Foddrell, P 1 1 2356
Clark, Myron Martin, C M 2 1 700
Clark, Rachel Clark, Ross 1 2 173
Clark, Robert Ly brook Clark, F L 1 1 10
Clark, Robert Nathaniel Clark, M F 1 1 18, 34
Clark, Thomas Clark, Ross 1 2 231
Clark, W. H. Clark, R L 1 2 120
Clark, Will Thompson, 1 2 81
Clark, W.T. ("Willie") Clark, Ross 1 2 231
Clemmons, Vaser Pendleton, B 1 1 192
Clifton, B.N. (Elder Bennie) Clifton, B.N. 1,4
Clifton, Elsie Cruise, C 1 2 117
Clifton, Fred Clifton, F taped all
Hopkins, E & B
Clifton, Levina Thomas, J 1 1 198
Clifton, Mae Clifton, F 1 2 277
Clifton, Tom Clifton, F 1 1 46
Clothmaking - Spinning, Thomas, J 1 1 144
Weaving, Clothes Williams, V 1 1 165
Strock, 1 1 328
Rakes, O 1 2 43
Barnard, W 2 2 365
Culler, C 1 1 116, 148
East, G 1 1 444 1 2 457, 465 2 2 550 21
Foley, R 1 2 320
Handy, L 1 1 114, 137

Homemade Harris, L 1 1 330
Washing Harris, O 1 1 105
Stores Helms, A & E 1 1 154
Houchins, M 3 1 274
Inscore, W R 1 2 137, 152
Jessup, L 1 2 111
Kendrick, J 1 1 95, 393
Pilson, O E 1 2 515
Shelor, B 1 1 63
Stuart, E S 1 1 330
Williams, W 1 1 295 1 3 163
Wood, A 1 1 272, 333
Wood, G & C 1 1 20, 70
Worley, L 1 1 214
Williams, D 3 2 116-134
Martin, C M 3 1 427 3 2 464 2 1 164
Rakes, O 2 1 244
Slate R & S 2 1 335, 352
Williams, W 1 2 119
Wood, A 1 2 440
Wood, G & C 2 1 300
Clark, M A 1 1 114
Fulcher, A 1 1 90
Handy, J & N 1 1 118 2 2 124, 137 3 2 138
Hopkins, W 1 1 128
Howell, R 1 1 72
Thompson, M E 2 2 220
Club Foot Pilson, A 1 2 188
Clubs, Civic, Organizations Williams, V 1 1 74
Rakes, O 1 1 71
Boaz, J 1 1 74
Hylton, B 1 1 132
Weaver, N 1 2 60
Coal Mining East, G 1 1 362
Hall, D 1 1 354
Williams, D 1 1 411 426 1 2 123, 132
Cockram, Alvis Clifton, F 1 1 210 22 1 2 134
Cockram, Babe Spangler, C 4 2 163
Bolt, 1 2 357
Cockram, Grover Cruise, C 1 2 117
Cockram, Jim Hopkins, E B 2 1 366

Fain, C 1 1 183
Cockram, Kitty Clyde (Spangler) Spangler, C 3 1 330
Cockram, Lane Shelor, F R 1 2 31
Cockram, Larkin Clifton, E N 1 2 33
Clifton, F 1 1 46, 210 1 2 134
Thomas, J 1 1 326 1 2 96
Cockram, Lilia Helms, 1 2 15
Cockram, Lizzie Hopkins, E & B 1 1 262
Cockram, Marvin Shelor, J R 1 2 31
Cockram, Rosa Hopkins, E B 1 1 341
Cockram School Hopkins, B & E 1 2 328
Collins, Mamie Barnard, W 1 1 141, 276
Combs, Minnie Mae (Walker) Hopkins, E & B 5 2 253
Commissioner of Revenue Thompson, M E 2 2 136 2 2 165
Commonwealth Attorney Clark, M F 3 1 202, 220, 240
Communications Inscore, W R 1 1 385, 400
Communities Turner, R M 2 2 185
Wood, G E 2 2 780
Community Life McKenzie, C & E 7 1 186
Spangler, D O 1 1 223
Inscore, W R 1 2 408
East, G 1 2 740. 764 23
Martin, C M 2 1 73, 81
Porter, R 2 2 172
Connor, Ellis Jessup, 2 1 70
Conner, Jonathan Barbour, 2 1 42
Conner, Mack Helms, 1 1 118
Conway, Joan Thompson, 1 1 364
Conway, "Kane" Hall, D 1 2 437
Conway, Lester Hall, D 1 2 437
Construction Barnard, W 1 1 224 2 1 39, 50
Clark, J M 3 1 54
Convicts, Convict Camps, Labor Hopkins, B & E 1 2 166
Hooker, J 1 1 190
Cook, Mary Hopkins, E B 5 2 70, 441
Cooking Barbour, A 2 2 595
Coolidge, Calvin Hooker, J 1 1 318
Cooper, Ben Terry, N R 1 1 43
Cooper, Benjamin Franklin Terry, N R 1 2 404
Cooper, Carlene (Cooper) Terry, N R 1 2 404
Cooper's Mill Terry, N R 1 1 118

Corn Martin, L & C 1 1 354
Corns, Sam Hardy, J & N
Corn Liquor Barbour, A 2 2 865
Corn Shucking Barbour, A 2 2 838
Hall, P 1 2 143
Fulcher, R & E 1 1 348
Layman, W 1 2 832
Mitchell, I 1 1 93
Pendleton, B 1 1 137 24
Pilson, O 2 2 765
Wood, A 1 2 118, 128
Kendrick, J 1 2 383
Martin, C M 2 2 565
Spangler, C 3 1 396
Wood, G &C 1 1 320, 390
Cosmetology Thompson, M E 2 2 350
Cotillion Dance Hopkins, B & E 4 1 171-345
Cotton Mills Thompson, M E 2 2 123
Counterfeiters Horton, L 2 1 39
Country Gentleman and Band Pendleton, B 1 2 392
Country Life Horton, L 3 1 350
Country Stores Barnard, W 1 1 241 3 1 57
Clifton, B 1 1 25
East, G 2 1 336, 344
Foddrell, M & T 1 1 210
Foley, R 1 1 35
Fulcher, R & E 1 2 370
Hall, D 1 1 86, 120
Handy, J & N 1 1 20
Harbour, K 1 1 96
Helms, A & E 1 1 39
Hopkins, B & E 1 1 195, 288
Howell, R 1 1 116 1 2 317
Hylton, B 1 1 29
Inscore, W R 1 1 30 1 2 230
Kendrick, J 1 1 257
Rakes, O 2 1 22
Shelor, B 1 2 345
2 1 72
Spangler, D O 1 1 78 1 2 90, 119
Stuart E S 1 1 195

Williams, V 1 1 28, 52
Wood, A 1 1 179, 185, 204
Wood, G & C 1 1 120
Country Stores Worley, L 1 1 32
Culler, C 1 1 37, 44 25
Cox W 2 1 360
Martin, C M 2 1 285
Tom Agee's Country Store Shelor, J R 1 2 241
County Administrators Clark, M F 2 1 150, 165
County Agents Clark, R L 1 2 86
County Fair Hopkins, B & E 5 2 88
Court Days Barnard, W 2 2 296, 307
Slate, R & S 4 2 312
Hooker, J 1 1 127, 354 3 1 390 3 2 45, 260
Thompson, M K 2 2 190
Courting Clark, J M 4 1 70
East, G 2 1 109
Fulcher, A W 1 2 225
Handy, J & N 1 2 235
Hopkins, L 1 1 320
Hopkins, W 1 2 97
Houchins, M 2 1 96
Howell, R 1 1 136
Mitchell, I 1 1 113-137
Penn, B 1 2 144
Strock, 2 1 301-382 2 2 21
Thompson, M K 1 2 34
Williams, V 1 2 477, 494
Wood, G & C 1 1 350
Worley, L 1 2 523
Cox, Conner Harris, L B 1 1 173
Cox, Henry Martin, E T 1 1 103
Cox, Lee Clifton, E N 1 1 137
Jessup, 2 1 27
Cox, William Odell, Sr. Cox, W O Sr. 1,2
Craddock, Harrison Slate, 1 2 116
Crafts Bolt, R 3 1 152 26
Howell, J 1 2 133
Patrick County HS 1 2 345
Crafts Stuart E S 1 1 299, 313
Slate, R & S 3 1 28

Creasy, Jack Slate, 4 1 134
Credit Foddrell, P 1 2 29
Crime Hooker, J 2 2 76
Houchins, L 4 2 40
Criminal Justice System Clark, M F 2 1 230, 250
Hooker, J 2 2 60 3 2 205
Critz Terry, W R 2 2 333
Layman, W 1 2 723
Martin, K 1 1 1 2
Grady, F & L 1 2 530
McKenzie, C & E 4 1 96
Martin, E 1 1 103, 133
Terry, N R 1 2 155 2 1 145, 155 2 2 167 2 2 265
Critz, Abe Carter, W C 1 1 240
Critz, Russell East, Gladys 2 2 466
Plaster, J 1 1 138
Terry, N R 2 1 98
Critz, William Dalton Martin, E T 1 2 757
Cruise, Crystal Cruise, C 1
Cruise, Frank Clifton, E N 1 1 137
Cruise, Levy Cruise, C 1 2 238 2 1 182
Cruise, Sam Hopkins, E & B 6 2 210
Cruise, Tex Fain, C 1 1 70
Cruise, Tina Pendleton Hopkins, E & B 1 1 98 27
Cub Scouts Horton, L 3 2 227
"Culture Shock" Hall, P 1 2 357
Cundiff, Dr. S.A. Spangler, D O 1 1 22
Cunningham, Clifford Layman 1 2 664
Dairies, Dairy Farming Cruise, C 1 2 256
Edwards, M 1 1 50
McKenzie, C & E 6 1 63
Martin, C M 2 2 730
Handy, J & N 2 2 177
Dalton, Clyde Carter, W C 1 1 240
Dalton, Crite Carter, W C 1 1 240
Plaster, J 1 1 138
Dalton, Frederick Pilson, A 2 1 129
Dalton, Hughes Fulcher, R & E 1 2 167
Dalton, John Pilson, A 2 1 129
Dances Foddrell, M & J 1 1 67 3 2 46
Square Dancing Hopkins 4 1 159

Cotillion Dancing Inscore, W R 2 2 376
Jessup, L 4 1 72
McAlexander, E 1 1 198
Martin, C M 2 2 467
Williams, D 1 2 231, 437 2 2 211, 246-312 3 2 229
Spangler, C 3 1 436 3 2 20
Foddrell, P 1 2 275
Wood, G E 3 1 212
Bolt, R 3 1 190
Daniel, W.C. "Dan" Terry, M A 1 1 79
Danube Church Barnard, W 1 1 123
Danville Barnard, W 3 1 257, 268 28
Clark, M A 2 2 321
Danville Bristol Turnpike Spangler, C 1 1 63, 83
Danville & Western Railway Boaz, J 1 2 687
Carter, W 1 1 180
Clark, J M 1 1 44 2 1 154
Clark, M A 1 2 254 2 2 35
Danville & Western Railway East, G 1 1 45, 68, 94, 124
1 2 563, 585, 592 2 1 225
Edwards, M 1 1 365
Hooker, J 1 1 141 2 1 37, 337 2 2 270-375
Hylton, B 1 2 338
Turner, J J 3 1 303 3 2 498, 645
Wood, G & C 1 1 100, 150
Wood, G E 1 2 791
Worley, L 1 2 618
Carter, W 1 2 755
Plaster, L 1 1 450
Carter, W 1 1 165 1 2 672-755
Martin, E 1 1 77, 182
Pilson, O 1 1 420
Carter, W 1 1 35. 123. 134, 240,290
East, G 2 1 200. 319
Layman, W 1 1 228
Martin, C M 1 1 80, 87, 138, 270 275, 378, 410, 435 1 2 546. 600 2 2
781
Carter, W 2 2 580
Martin, C M 3 1 187 3 2 912 1 1 410, 414 1 2 470, 490, 512, 643
Danville & Western Carter, W 1 1 260
Railroad Fulcher, A W 1 2 104

East, G 1 1 94
Layman, W 1 1 208, 325
Martin, C M 2 1 139
Plaster, J 1 1 51, 78, 85, 91 29
Carter, W 1 1 15, 110, 134 1 2 500, 565, 850 2 2 845
Plaster, J 1 1 111
Danville Wytheville Turnpike Clifton, F 1 1 450
Wood, A 1 1 58
Davis, Arthur Kyle McAlexander, 1 1 36, 370
Deal, Beverly Barbour, 2 1 315
Deaths Pilson, A 1 1 43, 270
DeBruhl, Gary Terry, M S 1 1 172
Debyns, Sam Slate, 1 1 210
DeHart, Charlie Clifton, F 1 2 134
Thomas, J 1 1 326
Wood, G & C 1 1 120
DeHart, Isaac C. Thompson, 2 2 246
Hooker, J 2 1 124
Spangler, C 4 1 250
DeHart, J. H. Weaver, 1 2 523
DeHart, Joe Thompson, 2 2 246
DeHart, Langhorne Spangler, C 4 2 268
DeHart, Leander Clifton, B N 1 1 25
Democratic Party Clark, M F 3 1 72
Dentists East, G 2 2 285
Fulcher, R & E 1 2 320
Jessup, L 1 1 398 2 1 2
Clark, R L 1 2 157
Fulcher, A W 1 2 46
Horton, L 3 2 184
Williams, D 3 1 219 3 2 39, 56
The Depression Barnard, W 1 23 117, 170 2 1 411, 440 30 3 1 84
Boaz J 1 1 215
Bolt, R 1 3 32, 54, 269, 280 2 1 56 3 1 152
Carter, W 1 1 152 2 1 200
Clark, J M 1 1 303
Clark, R L 1 1 285 1 2 86
Cox, W 2 2 216, 240, 275
Culler, C 1 1 390
East, G 2 2 466, 485
Edwards, M 1 1 195

Fain, C 1 1 418 1 2 29
Foddrell, M & T 1 2 175
Foley, R 1 2 305
Grady, F & L 1 1 443 1 2 464
Handy, J & N 1 1 311, 341 2 2 117
The Depression 3 2 32, 183
Harbour, K 1 2 646, 680
Harris, O 1 1 177
Hooker, J 2 1 57, 230-396
Hopkins, B & E 2 2 106 3 1 367
Hopkins, L 1 1 94, 363
Hopkins, W 1 2 157
Howell, R 1 1 290
Hylton, A H 1 1 256, 273
Hylton, B 1 1 250
Kendrick, J 1 2 145
McAlexander, E 2 1 206, 227
McKenzie, C & E 5 1 214
Plaster, L 1 1 45, 116-284
Rakes, O 1 1 274
Roberson, W 1 2 175
Shelor, B 2 2 50
Shelor, J & C 4 1 57
Spangler, D O 2 1 41, 59, 80, 110, 120 141, 181, 240, 300
Strock, 1 2 363
Thompson, M E 2 1 60
Williams, D 3 1 327, 337, 346
Wood, A 1 2 42
Wood, G E 3 1 5, 15, 32, 45, 50, 31, 85, 100, 123
Worley, L 1 1 382, 443 1 2 457
Hopkins, W 1 1 381
Martin, W 1 1 381
The Depression Clark, M A 1 1 273
Inscore, W R 1 1 343
Clark, R L 1 1 285
Cruise, C 1 2 198 2 1 182
Hall, D 1 1 331
Jessup, L 4 2 37, 38
Barbour, A 1 2 515 2 2 555
Williams, L 2 2 160
Harris, 1 2 2 85

Shelor, W A 1 1 23, 54
Mitchell, I 1 2 297
Pilson, A 1 1 204
Helms, A & E 1 1 265, 290
Slate, R & S 2 2 65
Dialects Bolt, R 3 1 35
Harris, L 2 2 132
Dickerson, Jim Thomas, J 1 1 378
Strock, 1 1 72
Dickerson, May Liza Houchins, 3 1 68
Dickerson, Meade Wood, A 2 2 392, 405
Diets Horton, L 3 2 144
Diphtheria Slate, R & S 1 1 301
Thompson, M E 3 1 383
Disabilities Horton, L 3 1 241
Discipline Fulcher, R & E 2 1 158
Discrimination, Blacks Houchins, M 1 1 133, 193
Penn, B 1 1 57
Women Terry, M S 3 1 228
Diseases Harris, L 1 2 151, 164
Pilson, A 1 2 159 32
Distilleries Clark, J M 1 1 85
Fain, C 1 2 418
Fulcher, A W 1 1 213
Hopkins, W 2 1 26
Jessup, L 3 2 81
Spangler, C 4 1 250-416
Thompson, M E 2 2 246
Weaver, N 1 1 207 1 2 523
Williams, D 2 1 354-437 2 2 36-89
Williams, W 1 1 315
Wood, G E 2 2 524, 545
Distilling, Illicit Boaz, J 1 1 108
Clark, M A 2 2 211
Cruise, C 1 2 48
Edwards, M 1 1 65
Foddrell, P 1 1 121, 135
Harbour, K 1 1 371
Hall, P 1 1 308
Helms, A & E 1 1 74
Hooker, J 2 2 129 2 1 373

Horton, L 2 2 109
Inscore, W R 2 1 62-385
Kendrick, J 1 2 64
Layman, W 1 2 838
Martin, L & C 1 1 44, 59, 88, 78, 102
Pilson, H 1 1 130
Rakes, O 2 1 75
Roberson, W 1 2 203
Spangler, C 3 2 137, 145, 382-455 4 1 20-290 4 2 375
Thompson, M E 2 2 259, 281
Weaver, N 1 1 198, 215, 235
Williams, W 1 2 291-455
Wood, G E 2 2 515, 545
Divers, Dr. Wood, G E 1 1 376
Divine Healing, Faith Healing Penn, B 1 2 290
Divining Rods, Dowsing Barnard, W 3 2 369
Divorce Barnard, J 1 1 384
Thompson, M E 1 2 350 33
Clark, M F 3 1 25
Dobyns Church Hall D 1 1 246
Dobyns, Mrs. Sam Harris, H P 1 1
Dobyns, S.G. Hall, D 1 1 97
Dobyns School Cruise, C 1 1 151
Doctors Barbour, A 2 2 636
Barnard, W 2 2 143, 159, 169 1 2 197 3 2 49
Bolt, R 2 1 131
Clark, R L 1 2 175
Cruise, C 2 1 445 2 2 7, 27
Culler, C 1 2 48, 55
East, G 1 2 807 2 2 598,608,733,829,880
Fain, C 1 2 319
Foley, R 1 2 319
Hall, D 1 2 204
Hall, P 1 2 176
Harris, H 1 2 525, 540
Horton, L 2 1 262
Penn, B 1 1 35
Pilson, A 1 1 5, 133, 148 1 3 176, 295
Shelor, J & C 3 2 43, 211, 276
Strock, 1 1 72
Thomas, J 1 2 1

Thompson, M E 2 1 455 2 2 24, 61
Turner, J J 1 2 526
Weaver, N 1 1 8
Williams, D 2 1 152, 185, 202-204 3 2 48
Williams, W 1 2 65
Wood, A 2 2 414
Wood, G & C 2 2 200
Wood, G E 1 1 321, 344, 376, 390 1 2 460
Dodson Hopkins, W 2 2 24
Dollarhite, Jim Slate, 4 1 134 34
Draft Barnard, W 1 2 178 3 2 198
Clark, M F 3 2 60
Spangler, D O 2 2 53, 119, 174
Williams, V 1 2 632
Dress, Clothing Style Houchins, M 4 2 166, 221
Drinking Shelor, W A 1 1 318
Weaver, N 1 1 240
Drought Barnard, W 3 2 180
Edwards, M 1 1 379
Helms, A & E 1 2 343
Mitchell, I 1 2 297
Pilson, A 1 1 195
Worley, L 1 2 597
Drownings Spangler, C 1 2 203
Druggist/Pharmacies Wood, G E 1 2 417 2 1 25
Drugs Patrick County HS 1 2 417 2 1 25
Drugs/Medication Harris, H 1 1 462 1 2 486, 640
Due Bills Handy, J & N 1 1 20
Wood, G & C 1 1 120
Duke Porter, P 2 1 27
Duncan, Will Clifton, F 1 1 276
Dunkley, Sam Clark, M A 2 1 140
Dyckes, Dr. J.W.H. McKenzie, 2 1 156 3 1 132
Dyeing, Clothes Howell, R 1 1 82
Jessup, L 3 1 139
East, Dump Carter, W C 1 1 269
East, Flora (Spencer) Wood, E M 1 1 54 35
East, Guy East, Gladys 2 1 200
Carter, W C 1 1 269
Easter Cruise, C 1 1 312
Economy Supply Co Layman, W W 1 1 224

Education Barnard, J 1 1 137
Clark, M F 1 1 78, 95, 230 1 2 218 2 1 25
Culler, C 1 2 185
Horton, L 1 2 163, 207, 212
Houchins, M 1 1 42, 128, 133 3 1 130
McKenzie, C & E 4 1 162 7 1 362
Pilson, O E 2 1 250
Spangler, D O 1 1 145 1 2 59, 81, 89 2 2 301
Spangler, C 2 1 278, 292, 307
Slate, R & S 1 1 188
Strock, 3 1 24 3 2 88, iii
Terry, N R 1 2 29
Turner, E M 1 1 80 1 2 300 2 2 88, 100, 115
Williams, D 1 1 391
Williams, L 1 2 98
Worley, L 1 2 767
Wood, E M 1 1 226
Edwards, Beulah Helms, 1 1 39
Edwards, Sharon Allen Edwards taped
Edward School Clifton, B 1 1 216
Eggleston, Kate (R.N.) East, Gladys 2 2 749
Eggleston, Mrs. Harris, H P 1 2 514
Elamsville Foley, R 1 1 35
Elamsville Methodist Church Roberson, W 1 1 251 36
Elections Hooker, J 1 1 299
Roberson, W 1 2 243
Slate, R & S 2 2 272
Thompson, M E 1 1 26, 48
Weaver, N 1 1 440, 470, 490
Wood, G & C 1 2 400, 490 2 1 20
Electricity Bolt, R 1 2 352
Clark, R L 1 2 264
East, G 1 2 791
Foley, R 1 1 178
Fulcher, A W 1 2 69
Fulcher, R & E 2 1 322
Grady, F & L 1 1 345, 357
Harris, O 1 1 214
Hopkins, B & E 3 1 438
Inscore, W R 1 1 327
Kendrick, J 1 1 91, 415

Layman, W 1 2 617-683
Martin, E 1 2 597, 838
Plaster, J 1 2 300, 345
Plaster, L 1 1 152
Spangler, C 4 2 168, 177, 189
Terry, N R 2 1 78
Weaver, N 1 1 392
Williams, V 1 2 460
Wood, A 1 2 353, 396
Wood, G & C 2 1 300
Emigration Spangler, C 3 1 71
Employment Barnard, J 1 1 219
Boaz, J 1 1 96, 154
East, G 1 1 362 2 1 134
Foddrell, M & T 1 1 199, 275, 334 1 2 163 3 1 324
Hall D 1 1 266
Hardin Reynolds E S 1 2 58, 100
Employment Helms, A & E 1 2 287
Kendrick, J 1 2 441
Patrick County HS 1 1 70, 190 2 2 96
Rakes, O 1 1 100
Stuart E S 1 2 287 37
Williams, D 2 1 224
Williams, W 1 1 275
Entertainment Barbour, A 2 2 487
Clark, J M 4 1 34, 446
East, G 1 1 377, 431
Foddrell, M & J 3 2 73
Fulcher, A W 1 1 109
Harris, O 1 1 97
Hooker, J 1 2 52
Inscore, W R 1 1 105 1 2 35, 47
Kendrick, J 1 2 197
Mitchell, I 1 1 57
Shelor, J R 1 1 182
Terry, W R 2 1 126
Wood, G & C 1 1 270
Worley, L 1 1 196
Epidemics, Flu and Diphtheria Cruise, C 2 2 27, 2
Thomas, J 1 2 285
Wood, A 1 2 242, 256, 279, 300

Wood, R A 1 1 198
Flu Handy, L 1 1 325
Shelor, B 2 1 170
Weaver, N 1 1 120
1918 Harris, L 1 2 164
Rakes, O 2 1 153
Epperson, Glen Barnard, W 2 1 255 2 1 154
Epperson, Inez Barnard, W 1 2 111 1 1 107
Equal Rights Amendment Terry, M S 3 1 204
Porter, P 2 2 34
Eubanks, Essie Strock, 1 2 211, 239
Evangelism McKenzie, C & E 2 1 94
Extension Homemakers Club Harris, L 1 2 180
Worley, L 1 1 142
Eyeglasses Houchins, M 1 2 262
Factories Cox, W 1 1 35, 70 38
Hooker, J 2 1 275
Spangler D O 1 2 274
Fain, Curtis R Fain, C 1
Fain, Holis Hopkins, E B 5 2 253
Fain, Ida Dollarhite Fain, C 1 1 70
Fain, Johnny Hall, D 1 2 259
Fairystone Cox, W 1 1 138, 375, 385 1 2 470
Fain, C 1 1 450
Hooker, J 2 1 255
Hopkins, W 1 2 200, 224
Kendrick, J 1 2 77
Turner, E M 2 2 22
Turner, J J 2 1 282
Fairystone Baptist Church McKenzie, C & E 2 1 182, 218
Families, Family Life, Reunions Edwards, M 1 1 45
Horton L 2 1 386
Rakes, O 2 1 107
Shelor, J & C 1 1 29
Williams, W 1 1 135, 149
Slate, R & S 2 1 300
Handy, L 1 2 170
Harbour, K 1 2 843
Harris, O 1 1 224
Helms, A & E 1 1 382 1 2 69
Inscore, W R 1 1 425

Barnard, J 1 1 91 1 2 212
Boaz, J 1 1 281,288,300,310,326
Bolt, R 3 2 35
Clark, M F 2 1 325, 370
Clifton, B 1 2 80
Harris, L 1 2 385 2 2 410
Horton, L 3 2 48, 250, 434
Howell, R 1 1 272 1 2 29, 63
Hylton, B 1 2 27
Martin, C M 2 2 539
Slate, R & S 1 2 148 39
Strock, 2 2 290 3 1 100-143, 228-252
Families, Family Life, Reunions Weavers, G 1 1 340
Williams, D 3 2 239
Williams, V 1 2 500, 533
Culler, C 1 2 129, 166
McAlexander, E 2 2 113
Thomas, J 1 2 180
Foddrell, M & T 2 1 75 3 2 120
Handy, L 1 2 283
Helms, A & E 1 2 62
Hopkins, B & E 6 2 93
Hylton, B 1 1 453 2 2 22
Penn, B 1 2 352
Pilson, A 2 1 250
Rakes, O 1 1 220
Shelor, J R 1 2 357
Williams, W 1 2 34
Wood, G & C 2 2 300, 338
Worley, 1 2 677
Farm Animals Howell, R 1 1 131
Inscore, W R 1 1 230
Shelor, J & C 1 1 70. 84
Farm Tractors Clark, R L 1 2 120
Farm Work Houchins, M 3 2 51
Farming Barbour, A 2 2 758
Barnard, W 1 1 64, 78 2 1 167 3 1 100 3 2 121
Bolt, R 1 1 280 2 1 56
Clark, J M 1 2 43
Clark, M A 1 1 37, 90, 125
Clark, R L 1 1 189

Clifton, B 1 1 159
Clifton, F 1 1 67, 149, 182
Cox, W 2 1 160
Edwards, M 1 1 156
Foley R 1 1 235, 308, 357
Fulcher R & E 1 1 49, 128
Grady, F & L 1 1 238, 253 40 1 3 647, 782 826, 850
Hall, D 1 1 132, 172
Hall, P 1 2 81
Handy, J & N 3 1 211-368
Handy L 1 1 35, 46
Farming Hardin Reynolds E S 1 1 66
Harris, L 1 1 39, 70 1 2 180
Helms, A & E 1 1 108
Hopkins, W 1 2 61
Horton, L 2 1 356 3 1 85
Houchins, M 1 2 24, 45
Inscore, W R 2 1 373, 409
Layman, W 1 2 548, 605
McKenzie, C & E 7 2 115
Martin, C M 3 2 769
Mitchell, J 1 2 202, 263
Patrick County HS 1 1 190
Pilson, A 1 1 238
Roberson, W 1 1 398
Shelor, B 1 1 33, 197
Spangler, D O 1 2 411 2 1 21
Thomas, J 1 1 299
Turner, E M 1 1 103, 128, 148, 173, 181, 205, 211
Turner, J J 1 1 218 2 2 512
Weaver, N 1 1 175
Williams, N 1 1 123, 285
Wood, A 1 2 18-134 2 1 118, 164
Wood, G & C 1 1 170 2 1 250
Wood, R A 1 1 169, 232, 245, 389
Pilson, O E 1 2 520 2 2 680
Land Slate, R & S 3 2 70
Chickens Shelor, J R 1 1 246
Corn Slate, R & S 1 2 61
Wood G E 2 1 284, 330
Depression Barnard, W 1 2 170

Planting Turner, J J 2 2 585
Wood, A 2 1 330, 409, 425
Self-sufficiency McAlexander, E 2 1 49, 101
Sheep 2 1 49 41
Terracing Slate, R & S 5 1 22
Fayerdale Clark, R L 1 1 237
Hall, P 1 1 86
Carter, W 1 1 317
Railroad Hall, P 1 1 86
Hopkins, W 1 2 262
Pilson, A 1 2 239
Roberson, W 1 2 153
Turner, J J 3 1 395
Fayerdale Weaver, N 1 2 523. 540
Turner, J J 1 1 322, 347 1 2 400
Feathers, Ducks, Geese Fulcher, A W 1 2 150
Williams, W 1 2 199
Fellowship Federated Church Porter, P 1 1 124
Ferrum College Cruise, C 1 1 438 1 2 1
Hall, P 1 1 156
Roberson, W 1 2 163
Wood, E M 1 2 799
Feuds Spangler, C 4 2 320-353
Fiddle Makers Pendleton, B 1 2
Fieldcrest Mills Martin, C M 1 2 730
Foddrell, M & T 3 2 331
Finnes, Joe Houchins, 3 1 125
Fires, Fire Dept, Rescue Squads Turner E M 2 2 200 1 1 389
Worley, L 1 2 643
Fires East G 1 2 683
Martin, L & C 1 2 523, 572, 596
Helms, A & E 1 2 237
Layman, W 1 2 484
Fireplaces Horton, L 1 1 139, 262 1 2 43
Inscore W R 2 2 260, 274
McKenzie, C & E 6 2 162
Worley, L 1 1 251 42
Fires Wood G E 1 1 46, 95 3 2 602, 628
Wood, G & C 2 2 100, 150
Fishing Barnard, W 1 2 329
Cruise, C 2 1 323

Handy, J & N 2 2 365
Horton, L 3 1 43
Five Forks Handy, J & N 3 1 20, 120, 420
Flatt, Lester Shelor, J R 1 2 1
Flax Weaving Shelor, B 1 1 72
Flippin, Jess Thompson, 3 2 30
Clark, M A 1 2 223
Flippin, Jesse Hopkins, E & B 2 1 97
Floods Fain, C 1 2 294
Foddrell, P 1 1 403
Rakes, O 1 1 362
Flood of '79 Turner, E M 1 1 389 2 1 82, 267, 367
Foddrell, Marvin Foddrell, P 1 2 300
Foddrell, M & T 1-4
Foddrell, Posey L Foddrell, 1
Foddrell, Turner Foddrell, P 1 2 300
Foddrell, M & T 1-4
Foddrell, Sarah Jane Foddrell, P 1 1 161
Foley, Matt Pilson, A 1 2 95
Foley, Robert Earl Foley, R E 1
Foley, Zarder Pilson, A 1 2 229
Food Grady, F & L 1 1 277
East, G 1 1 444 1 2 457
Kendrick, J 1 1 257
Inscore, W R 1 2 130 43
Wood, A 2 2 231
Diet Houchins, M 2 1 234 2 2 130
Wood, G E 2 1 88,105 3 2 830
Wood, G & C 1 1 170,390
Prep Bolt, R 2 1 162
East, G 1 1 83
Fulcher, A W 1 2 425
Handy, J & N 3 2 286-369
Martin, C.M. 3 1 40 3 2 546
Shelor, B 1 1 57 2 1 54
Strock, 2 2 61
Williams, D 3 2 256, 283
Williams, V 786
Wood, G E 3 2 804
Cornmeal Slate, R & S 4 1 380
Cooking Raccoon Hall, D 1 2 12

Bolt, R 1 1 388
Fulcher, A W 1 1 379, 403 1 2 373
Fulcher, R & E 1 2 33
Handy, J & N 3 2 394
McKenzie, C & E 7 1 113
Martin, C.M. 3 1 397
Martin, L & C 1 1 323 1 2 536
Mitchell, I 1 1 178
Pilson, A 1 1 311
Slate, R & S 2 1 149, 160
Thomas, J 1 1 135
Food Preservation Wood, A 2 2 241, 305
Wood, G E 2 1 195 3 2 830
Canning Culler, C 1 1 179
Supplies Martin, C M 2 1 238, 245, 267
Williams, D 3 2 256, 283
Foot Washing Roberson, W 1 1 251
Forbes, Patrick McKenzie, 2 2 224
Foreigners Buying Land Barnard, W 3 1 401 44
Forest Fires Martin, L & C 1 2 572, 596
Wood, G E 3 2 555
Forests Farming McKenzie, C & E 7 2 127
Fort Mayo (French & Indian War) Turner, J J 3 1 35
Foster, Aubrey Carter, W E 2 1 135
Foster, Howard Pendleton, B 1 1 183, 192
Foster, Penn Carter, W C 1 1 269
Fourth of July Inscore, W.R. 1 2 218
Shelor, B 2 1 271
France, Joseph Peter Turner, J J 1 2 675
Freeman, Walter Carter, W C 1 1 290
Free State of Patrick Clark, L L 1 2 218
Clark, M F 1 2 18, 25, 65, 95 2 1 390
Hylton, B 1 2 310
Terry, N R 2 2 68
Free Union School Clifton, B 1 1 216
Shelor, B 2 1 132
Thomas, J 1 1 198 1 2 370
Wood, A 1 1 405
Frugality Layman, W 1 2 586
French & Indian War Turner, J J 1 2 780
Fugate, Mary Catherine McKenzie, 1 1 177

Fulcher, Albert Rush Fulcher, R & E 1,2
Fulcher, Alice West Fulcher, A 1
Fulcher, Henry Fulcher, R & E 1 2 320
Fulcher, Lula Ann Wood, E M 1 1 39 45
Fulcher, Ora Belle (Martin) Martin, C M 1 1 49
Fulcher, Rachel Edith (Martin) Fulcher, R & E 1,2
Fulcher, Shadie Layman, 1 1 80
Fulcher, Verta Layman, 1 1 412
Fuller, Blind Boy Foddrell, M & T 1 1 181
Fulton, Waite "Capt" Carter, W C 1 1 240, 290
Fulton, W.P, "Bill" Clark, R L 3 1 386
Funerals Barnard, W 1 2 188
Clark, M A 1 2 125
Culler, C 1 2 221, 226
East, G 1 2 848
Fain, C 1 2 142
Foddrell, P 1 1 161
Fulcher, A W 1 1 427 1 2 20
Handy, J & N 1 2 146
Harris, L 2 1 33, 105
Layman, W 1 2 785
McAlexander, E 2 2 89
Funerals McKenzie, C & E 1 2 188
Penn, B 1 1 429
Plaster, L 1 2 685
Slate R & S 2 1 133
Spangler D O 1 2 211
Strock, 1 1 408, 435 2 1 150-194
Thomas, J 1 2 13
Thompson, M E 3 2 105
Weaver, N 1 1 60, 73
Williams, W 1 1 91
Wood, A 1 2 211, 229
Wood, G E 2 2 615, 644, 670, 705, 760
Furniture, Handmade Martin, E 1 2 850
Pilson, A 1 1 168
Factories Handy, L 1 1 143
Martin, C M 1 2 600, 643, 670
Harris, L 1 1 142, 166
Hall, P 1 2 382
Harris, O 1 2 570 46

Games (Toys, Marbles, Croquet) Cruise, C 1 1 48
Fulcher, R & E 2 1 69, 84
Hall, P 1 1 319
Handy, J & N 1 2 29
Harris, L 1 1 242
Hopkins, B & E 2 2 236 3 2 147
Roberson, W 1 1 196
Spangler, C 2 2 369
Stuart E S 1 1 69, 98, 121
Worley, L 1 1 178
Foley, R 1 1 419 2 1 35
Bolt, R 1 2 143, 185, 312
McAlexander, E 2 1 330
McKenzie, C & E 1 1 24
Shelor, J & C 3 1 190-456 3 2 1
Plaster, J 1 2 7
Gardening Pilson, A 1 2 418
Slate, R & S 4 1 257
Gasoline Grady, F & L 1 2 896
Gates, Mrs. John Inscore, 2 2 300
Gardner, Bemm Spangler, C 3 2 382
Gardner, Olen Pendleton, B 1 2 80
George, Brooks Clark, L 1 2 160
George, Thomas J. ("Tom", T.J.) Slate, 1 1 51
Clark, M A 2 1 35
George Plasters Store Martin, C M 2 1 146
George T Horne & Co Hopkins, B & E 1 1 273
Ghosts Barnard, W 2 1 220, 239, 294
Fain, C 1 1 316
Hall, D 1 2 75
Handy, L 1 2 95
Horton, L 2 2 26, 39
Inscore, W R 1 1 390
Mitchell, I 1 1 390 47 1 2 28-170
Turner, J J 3 2 875
Williams, D 3 1 290
Gibson, Charley Dancy Spangler, C 1 1 386
Gibson Girls Spangler, C 1 1 386
Gilbert, Lemly Thomas, J 1 1 378
Gilbert, Noel Thomas, J 1 1 378
Glaucoma "Langhorn Disease" Spangler, C 1 1 178, 218

Glenn, Robert Penn, B 1 1 169
Goad, Edna M.H. Walker Church 1 1 32
Goad, Marie M.H. Walker Church 1 1 21
Goblintown Hall, P 1 2 60
Goin, Grover Horton, 1 1 140
Gold Mines Plaster, J 1 1 328
Goode, Joe Houchins, 2 1 125 3 1 379
Goode, Virgil Turner, E M 2 2 225
Goodrich, Eva Barnard, 1 1 141
Goodwill Church of the Brethren Roberson, W 1 1 251
Government Hylton, B 1 2 222
Clark, M F 2 1 165 1 2 145, 160, 167, 198, 230 2 1 10, 135, 350, 435 2 2 205, 245, 260
Hooker, J 3 2 125
Terry, N R 1 1 245
McKenzie, C & E 7 1 422 7 2 25
Turner, E M 1 1 233
Clark, J M 2 2 201 48
Clark, M F 2 1 54, 115 1 2 65, 88 2 2 40
McKenzie, C & E 7 2 64
Turner, E M 1 2 233 2 2 215
Hopkins, W 2 2 369
Grady, Luch & Frank Grady tape
Grafton, Ernestine Clark, L 1 2 267
Grandparents Hopkins, B & E 3 2 58
Grapes Slate, R & S 4 1 314
Grawly, R.P. Pilson, O E 3 2 895
Green Hill Church Hopkins, B & E 3 1 169
Thompson, M E 3 1 111
Green, Sammy Terry, N R 1 2 261
Greenhill Baptist Church Fain, C 1 1 172
Greenwood School Clifton, F 1 1 210
Griffith, Martha (Congresswoman) Terry, M S 1 1 85
Griggs, Arch Carter, W C 1 1 353
Griggs, John Grady, 1 1 477
Grogan, Mabel Grady, 1 1 72
Gum Swamp School Helms, A & E 1 2 35
Guns Wood, R A 1 2 156
Gunsmiths Shelor, J & C 4 1 176 4 2 1
Gypsies Clark, J M 4 1 176
Fulcher, R & E 1 2 77 49

Haggar, Della Wood Houchins, 2 1 151
Hairston, (Col.) George Turner, J J 3 1 102
Hairston, John Martin, C M 1 1 176
Hall, Cecil Pendleton, B 1 1 239
Hall, Henry Harden Hall, P 1 1 30 1 2 30
Hall, James Slate, on tape catalog only 4 1 80
Hall, Jennie Wood, R A 1 1 24
Hall, Joel Spangler, C 4 2 400
Hall, Martha Elizabeth Ross Hall, P 1 1 30
Hall, Miss Harris, H P 1 2 514
Hall, Pearl Lillian Hall, P 1
Hall, Wade Clifton, F 1 1 317
Halloween Thompson, M E 1 1 59, 80
Williams, D 2 1 82
Hamilton, W.W. Wood, G E 1 1 120
Hamm, Mack Hall, D 1 1 122
Handy, Mrs. Babe Strock, 2 1 28
Handy, Ed Hall, D 1 2 259
Handy, Ernest Handy, J & N 1 1 45
Handy, George B. Handy, J & N 1 2 70
Handy, John Preston Handy, J & N 1,2,3
Handy, Lilla Shelor Handy, L S 1
Handy, Murry Foddrell, P 1 1 263
Handy, Novella Stevens Handy, J & N 1,2,3 50
Handy, Soloman Clifton, E N 1 1 137
Handy, Spangler Hall, D 1 2 437
Handy, Will Handy, L S 1 1 84
Handy, Zula Terry, M S 1 2 117
Handy's Store Hall, D 1 1 80
Harbour, Clara Kendrick, 1 1 53
Harbour, Delores Foley, R E 1 1 52, 119
Harbour, Kenneth Green Harbour Tape
Harbour School Pilson, A 1 1 96 2 1 270
Hardin Reynolds School Layman W 1 2 546
Martin E 1 2 517
Plaster J 1 2 81
Pilson O 1 2 617
Roberson W 1 1 30
Terry M S 1 2 57
Harmon, Dr. Jim Weaver, N 1 1 5
Harrell, Dorsey Wood, A 1 2 353

Harris, Bootie Shelor, J & C 1 2 152
Harris Chapel School Howell, R 1 1 181
Harris, Hallie Pace Harris, H 1 1 32, 40, 55, 74, 373
Harris, Harve Bolt, 1 2 352
Harris, John Jessup, 2 2 178
Harris, Lee (Mr. & Mrs.) Foley, R E 1 1 119
Harris, Linda (Surratt) Harris, O 1 2
Harris, Math Bolt, 1 2 352
Harris, Oscar Allen Harris, O 1 51
Harris, (Capt.) Samuel Turner, J J 3 1 53
Harvey, E.J. (Judge) Thompson, 2 2 190
Hash, Nannie Hopkins, E & B 2 1 366
Hatcher, Annie M. (Mrs. W.H.) Weaver, G 1 1 487
Hatcher, Mrs. Ben Hall, D 1 2 110
Hatcher, Claude Houchins, 1 2 85
Hatcher, Ham Martin, C M 1 1 190
Hatcher, Hamp Fain, C 1 2 184
Hatcher, Orie Strock, 1 1 79
2 1 180
Haunted Houses Hall, D 1 2 317, 329
Hayden, Ben Martin, C M 1 1 237
Carter, W C 1 1 240
Haynes, Mary Hopkins, E & B 5 2 200
Hay Rides Clark, J M 4 1 118
Healers Hall, D 1 2 122
Health (Diet) Handy, L 1 1 292
Heath, Caleb Slate, 1 1 62
Heating Systems Barnard, W 3 2 297, 309
Bolt, R 1 2 385
Martin, C M 3 2 527
Heidebach Mission School
Roberson W 1 1 90
Helms, Abraham H. & Eula Helms 1 Tape 1
Helms, Abraham Madison Helms 1 2 15
Helms, George Helms, 1 1 316
Helms, John Horton, 1 1 88 52
Hensley, Ben Clifton, F 2 2 277
Hensley, Frances Hopkins, E & B 5 2 226
Herbs Handy, L 1 1 80
Wood, G & C 2 1 100, 150
Williams, D 3 1 181, 194, 388, 397

Highway Department Hopkins, B & E 2 2 168
Hill, Bessie Barnard, W 1 1 141
Hill, Clarence & Henry Pendleton, B 1 2 155
Hines, Morgan Hylton, A 1 1 170
Hines, Sandy Hylton, A 1 1 200
Hipps, James Pendleton, B 1 2 155
Hitchhiking Pilson, O 1 2 692
Hodges, Charlie Fain, C 1 1 70
Hodges, Ellen Strock, 3 2 403
Hog Butchering/Farming Harris, L 2 1 225
Kendrick, J 1 2 350
Martin, C M 2 2 649
Slate, R & S 4 2 170
Thompson, M E 2 1 99
Wood, A 2 2 241
Wood, G & C 1 1 220
Terry, N R 1 1 173
Wood, R A 1 1 441
Weaver N 1 1 310
Holidays Fulcher, A W 1 2 127
Williams, D 2 1 326
Holy Land Pilson, O 3 1 210
Home Demonstration Clubs Hopkins, B & E 4 1 332
Home Remedies (See Herbs) Barnard, W 2 2 109
Clark, R 1 2 431
Cruise, C 2 2 2, 69 53
East, G 2 2 652, 666, 672
Fain, C 1 2 115
Foley, R 1 2 108
Fulcher, A W 1 1 178
Hall, D 1 2 137
Home Remedies (See Herbs) Hardy, L 1 2 35
Horton, L 2 1 250
Houchins, M 2 1 29
Jessup, L 2 2 3
Martin, L & C 1 1 405
Shelor, J & C 3 2 32
Slate, R & S 3 1 266
Williams, D 2 1 132, 144 3 1 181, 194, 338, 397
Wood, G & C 2 1 100
Wood, G E 1 2 511 2 1 206

Martin, L & C 1 1 405
Foddrell, P 1 1 235
Harris, L 2 1 53
Hominy Thomas, J 1 1 104
Honesty Clark, J M 1 2 134 4 1 242, 298
Foddrell, P 1 2 137
Honey, Bee Keeping Slate, R & S 3 1 92 4 1 201
Hooker, Annie Dillard Hooker, J D 1 2 371
Hooker, Billy Clark, R L 1 2 386
Hooker, Elizabeth (Bailey) Hooker, J D 2 1 218 3 2 400
Hooker, Gordon Horton, 1 1 73
Hooker, W. Lester (Judge) Hooker, J D 1 1 331
Barnard, W 2 2 323
Clark, L 1 2 160
Clark, M F 1 1 330
Hooker, J. Murray Hooker, J D 1 1 117, 271 3 1 14
Clark, R L 1 2 386
Hooker, J D 3 2 365
54
Hooker, (Judge) John Dillard Hooker, J D 1-3
Clark, L 1 2 160
Clark, M F 3 1 68
Hopkins, Betsy Hughes Hopkins, E & B 6 2 118
Hopkins, Beulah, (Mrs. Early) Hopkins, E & B 1-7
Terry, N R 1 2 261
Hopkins, Brewster Dr. Hopkins, E & B 1 1 235
4 2 54
7 2 426
Hopkins, Early Hopkins, E & B 1-7
Hopkins, Early R. Jr. Hopkins, E & B 4 1 375
Hopkins, Emily Louette (DeHart) Hopkins, E & B 1 1 62
Hopkins, James Daniel Hopkins, E & B 1 1 70 2 2 53
Hopkins, Harley Ray Hopkins, E & B 1 1 235 4 1 365
Hopkins, James Walter Hopkins, E & B 4 1 383
Hopkins, Jim Clifton, F 1 2 134
Hopkins, Joseph E. Hopkins, E & B 2 2 79 Pilson, A 1 1 123
Hopkins, Mildred Terry, N R 1 2 261
Hopkins, Rosa Hopkins, E & B 5 1 410
Hopkins, Rosa Elizabeth Hopkins, E & B 1 1 67, 235
Hopkins, Sammie Green McKenzie 6 2 290
Hopkins, Walter Thomas Dudley

Hopkins, W T D 1 -
Hopkins, E & B 1 2 35
Horne, Chevis McKenzie, 2 1 201
Horner, Mary (Walker) Hopkins, E & B 5 2 226, 253 55
Horses Shelor, J & C 1 1 95-162, 280 2 2 281, 341
Terry, N R 2 1 196
East, G 2 1 415
Clark, J M 4 1 224
Clark, R 1 1 341
Hopkins, W 2 1 256
Horton, James Aubrey Horton, 2 1 108
Horton, Larry P. Horton Tapes 1,2,3
Horton, Marion Horton, 2 1 117 2 2 359
Hospitals Clark, M A 2 2 134
Clark, R L 1 2 175
Fain, C 1 2 319
Hall, D 1 2 204
Harris, H 1 1 1 2
Plaster, J 1 1 185, 206
Thomas, J 1 2 266
Thompson, M E 2 1 455 2 2 24, 61, 89
Wood, G E 1 1 344
Penn, B 1 1 24
Hotels Clark, J M 2 1 382
Clark, M A 1 2 35
East, G 1 1 150
Houchins, Lizzie Roberson, W 1 2 66
Housing/Houses Wood, A 1 2 128 2 2 145
Wood, G & C 1 2 300
Hardin Reynolds E S 1 2 300
Howell, R 1 1 64
Barnard, W 1 1 284
Harbour, K 1 2 753
Hopkins, B & E 2 2 73
Layman, W 1 2 906
Martin, E 1 2 213
Shelor, B 1 2 297
Strock, 1 1 24-62, 96 1 2 107
Wood, E M 1 2 664 56
Rakes, O 2 1 303
Slate, R & S 1 1 25, 62, 75, 210

Handy, L 1 1 190
Horton, L 1 1 50-302
Bolt, R 1 2 56 2 1 225
Clark, M A 1 1 72
Harris, L 1 1 142
Culler, C 1 1 160
Howard, William Wood, G E 1 2 669
Howell, Elijah Hopkins, E & B 1 1 421
Howell, Hugh Hooker, J 2 1 275
Howell, Jeff Cruise, C 1 2 117
Howell, Ruby Underwood Howell Tape 1 1
Howell, W.P. Clifton, F 1 1 46
Hubbard, Burrell Clifton, F 1 1 46
Hubbard, Clabe Clifton, F 1 1 46
Hubbard, Juel or Burl Spangler, C 3 1 120
Hubbard, Millie M.H. Walker Church 1 1 203
Hubbard, Webb Jessup 1 2 289
Hughes, "Arch" Hylton, V 1 2 245
Hughes, Archiles Pilson, O E 4 2 550
Humor Bolt, R 3 2 78, 95, 208
Hundley, Dick Carter, W C 1 1 260
Hundley, Hassell Carter, W C 1 1 269
Hunters Chapel Porter, P 1 1 124, 147
Hunting Boaz, J 1 1 336
Bolt, R 3 1 400
Edwards, M 1 1 80, 104, 148
Foley, R 1 1 324 57
Hall, D 1 1 413 1 2 1
Handy, J & N 1 1 346 1 2 79
Harris, O 1 1 262
Helms, A & E 1 2 98
Hopkins, B & E 6 2 357
Horton, L 2 1 148
Howell, R 1 2 333
McKenzie, C & E 5 1 258
Pilson, O 2 2 780
Shelor, J R 2 1 112
Weaver, N 1 1 560
Williams, D 1 2 33 2 2 151 3 1 309
Williams, V 1 2 544
Worley, L 1 2 529

Clark, R 1 1 376
Shelor, J & C 3 2 344
Wood, A 2 1 22-77
Hunting Wood, G & C 2 1 200
Wood, R A 1 2 230
Foxes East, C 2 1 238
Fishing Harbour, K 1 3 738
Hutchens, Evelyn Spangler, C 2 2 20
Hylton, Annie Hines Hylton, A I tape 1
Hylton, Valentine Staples Hylton, B 1 1 2 2
Hylton, Wade Slate, 3 2 140
Spangle, C 4 2 265
Williams, D 2 1 116
I M Akers Store Hopkins, W 1 1 113
McKenzie, C & E 5 2 42
Weaver, N 1 1 280
Ice Cream Wood, G E 2 1 59
Ice Houses Martin, C M 2 1 383
Thompson, M E 3 1 153, 171
Williams, D 2 2 172
Wood, G E 1 2 582 2 1 59, 72, 78 58
Immunizations Fain, C 1 2 383
Indian Knob School
Black School Hylton, A H 1 1 390
Indians Spangler, C 1 2 297
Barnard, W 1 1 33 2 2 385
Pilson, O 3 2 755
Turner, J J 1 2 840 2 1 29
Industrialization Clark, M F 1 1 360, 380,425 1 2 3 2 1 404
Turner, E M 2 1 42
Foddrell, M & T 3 2 390
Industry Hardin Reynolds E S 1 2 25
Hopkins, B & E 3 2 389
Stuart E S 1 1 217, 244
Thompson, M E 1 2 251 2 2 123
Infants Strock, 2 2 22-67
Inman, Deck Jessup, 2 1 104
Inscore, Russell Inscore
Inscore's Grocery Inscore, W R 2 2 97
Insects Mitchell, I 1 1 188-232
Integration Hylton, A H 1 1 128

Iron Bell School Houchins, M 1 1 128 1 2 154
Iron Mine (Fayerdale) Turner, J J 3 2 736
Hopkins, W 1 2 262
Plaster, J 1 1 223
Ironing, Housework Slate, R & S 2 2 431
Isolation Clifton, F 1 2 258
JEB Stuart Dedication Weaver, G 1 1 135 59
JEB Stuart Woman's Club Clark, L L 1 1 93 1 2 205
J P Stevens Co Boaz, J 1 2 724
Clark, M A 2 2 321
Handy, J & N 1 2 120
Harbour, K 1 1 186, 352
Helms, A & E 1 1 65 1 2 349
Martin, C M 1 2 700
Rakes, O 1 1 65
Roberson, W 1 1 380
Spangler, D O 1 2 397, 411
Weaver, N 1 2 130
Hylton, A H 1 1 312
Jackson, Tommy Pendleton, B 1 2 185
Japan Weaver, N 1 2 258, 288, 335, 385
Jessup, Alice Jessup, 2 2 178, 237
Jessup, Ceph Jessup, 1 2 372
Jessup, Delsie Jessup, 1 1 189
Jessup, Eligie Jessup, 1 1 185
Jessup, George Jessup, 1 2 289, 372 2 1 360 4 2 108
Jessup, Hilory Jessup, 2 1 117, 129
Jessup, Lula Emaline (Lynch) Jessup tapes 1 1
Jessup, Sam Jessup, 2 2 126
Jessup, Virgil Jessup, 2 1 208
Jesus Christ Terry, M S 4 1 50
Jimmy Lee Via's Store Martin, E 1 1 242
Johnson, Akers Strock, 1 2 490 60
Johnson, John Barnard, W 1 2 154
Joyce, Aubrey Slate, 1 1 244
Joyce, Cara Genter Thomas, J 1 1 198
Joyce, Dana Martin, Callie 1 2 674
Joyce, Evelyn Hylton, A 1 1 420
Joyce, Will Foddrell, P 1 2 150
Joyce and Shelton Store Layman, W 1 1 100, 163
Martin, C M 2 1 302

East, G 1 2 683
Justice Terry, M S 2 1 171
Justice of the Peace Hull, P 1 1 30
Hooker, J 3 1 205
Juvenile, Domestic Court
Hooker, J 3 1 330
Clark, M F 2 1 258, 265, 275, 290 2 2 180
Kahan, Ann Clark, L L 1 2 92
Kendrick, Edgar Barbour, A 1 1 155
Kendrick, Jesse E. Kendrick, J tape 1 1
Kerosene Lamps Fulcher, R & E 2 1 193
Kerosene Lamps Hopkins, B & E 1 2 313
Wood, R A 1 1 282
Kibler Valley Barnard, W 1 1 197, 402 3 1 33
Horton, L 3 1 25 3 2 451
Williams, L 1 2 280, 436
Kirk, David Hopkins, E & B 4 2 112
Knitting Strock, 1 3 188
Shelor, J & L 1 1 210, 256
Korean War Howell, R 1 1 388 61
Lady Astor - Langhorne Spangler, C 1 1 348, 379
Lancaster, (Dr.) Albert Hall, P 1 1 86 1 2 176
Land Slate, R & S 4 1 222
Hylton, B 1 2 403
Spangler, C 2 2 170, 195
Bolt, R 2 1 335
Spangler, C 1 2 20, 30, 84
Stuart, E S 1 2 225
Landowners - Patrick Springs Martin, C M 2 2 790
Langhorne, Chiswell Spangler, C 1 1 348
Langhorne, James Steptoe Spangler, C 1 1 256 2 1 20, 39, 59
Langhorne, William Spangler, C 2 2 62
Lature, Rupert Hopkins, E & B 5 2 23
Laundry Mitchell, I 1 1 254-290
Law Enforcement Wood, G E 2 2 467, 477, 492, 511
Law Practice Clark, M F 1 2 275, 290 3 1 60, 260
Hooker, J 1 2 400 2 1 160
Terry, M S 2 1 171
Law School Clark, M F 1 1 197, 220, 260, 278
Terry, M S 3 1 130
Lawn Parties McKenzie, C & E 1 1 50

Lawyers Hooker, J 1 1 375
Layman, Ray Layman, 1 2 664
Layman, Raymond Wood, E M 1 1 207
Layman, W. Edgar Layman Tape 1 1
Leadership Clark, M F 1 2 167, 180, 242 62 2 1 435
Turner, E M 1 2 98
Leather Craft Barnard, W 1 2 146
Legon, Will Hall, D 1 2 437
Leonard, Georgia (Moore) Wood, E M 1 2 842
Lester, Sandy Hylton, A 1 2 12
Lewis, Jim Clifton, E N 1 1 137
Clifton, F 1 2 277
Lewis, Perry Barber, 1 1 191
Lewis, Roy Barber, 1 1 290 1 2 475, 766
Lewis, Wilmoth (Mrs. William R.) Clark, R L 1 2 330
Liberty School Kendrick, J 1 1 53
Pilson, O 1 2 830
Library of Congress Barnard, W 3 1 66
Lifestyles Fain, C 1 2 63
Foddrell, M & T 1 1 240
Horton, L 1 1 314 3 2 355
Turner, E M 1 2 370
Clark, J M 2 1 235 4 1 341
Clark, M A 1 2 49, 166 2 2 291
Hall, D 1 2 359
Pilson, H 1 1 99
Weaver, N 1 1 392, 410
Light, Kale Jessup, 4 1 242
Lighting Strock, 3 1 423
Hopkins, W 1 2 138
Martin, C M 2 1 142
Thompson, M E 1 2 190
Wood, G & C 2 2 50, 100 63
Liquor Williams, D 3 2 88, 100
Livery Stables Layman, W 1 1 51, 66
Thompson, M E 1 1 422 2 1 51, 64
Weaver, G 1 1 51
Livestock Wood, A 2 1 180, 210
Living Conditions/Standards Martin, L & C 1 1 271 1 2 852
Thompson, M E 2 1 40
Log Rollings Hopkins, B & E 7 1 177

Jessup, L 3 1 326
Spangler, C 3 2 60, 77
Logging Clifton, B 1 1 54, 77, 88
Love, Gaston Barnard, W 2 1 200
Lovers Leap Shelor, J & C 4 1 90
Lumber/Lumber Business Slate, R & S 1 1 383
Layman, W 1 1 274
Williams, V 1 1 106 1 2 640
Luray Caverns Hopkins, B & E 2 2 412 3 1 24
Lybrook, Sam Clifton, F 1 1 67
Spangler, C 3 1 139
Lynch, Bob Jessup, 2 1 208
Lynch, Brooks Jessup, 1 1 150
Lynch, Frank Jessup, 4 1 273
Lynch, John Jessup, 1 1 123, 336
Jessup, 4 1 287
Lynch, Ruffin Jessup, 1 1 24 2 1 229
Lynch, Sam Jessup, 2 2 92 64
Lynch, Wilburn Bolt, 1 1 63
Mabe, John Martin, C M 2 2 480
Magistrates Slate, R & E 4 2 312
Mail Carriers Fain, C 1 2 307
Fulcher, A W 1 2 81
Hall, D 1 1 97
Hopkins, B & E 1 2 22
Hopkins, W 2 1 64, 122, 290 2 2 24-158
Layman, W 1 1 255
Martin, E 1 2 625
Roberson, W 1 2 100
Shelor, J & C 1 1 162 2 2 255
Spangler, C 3 1 250
Thomas, J 1 2 323
Wood, A 1 1 152
Wood, R A 1 2 244
Wood, G E 3 1 369, 434
Pilson, O 1 1 115
Mail Order Stores Hopkins, B & E 7 1 296
Mail Service Clark, R L 1 2 220
Man Who Moved a Mountain Williams, L 3 2 35
Mann, Robert McKenzie, 2 1 163
Mann Stovall's Mill Martin, C M 2 2 600

Manners - Children Penn B 1 2 194
Manor, Mack Layman, 1 2 643
Marriage - Separations Barnard, J 1 1 384 1 2 30
Cruise, C 1 2 155
Fulcher, B & E 1 2 267
Harris, O 1 2 710
Hopkins, B & E 7 2 25
Hopkins, L 1 1 320
Hylton, B 1 3 27, 90
Inscore, W R 2 1 161 65
Jessup, L 2 2 178
Mithcell, 1 1 1 137
Marriage Pilson, A 2 1 21-78
Porter, P 1 2 182 2 1 217, 407
Thompson, M E 1 2 350
Wood, G E 3 2 694
Spangler, P O 1 2 240
Williams, D 2 1 95
Wood, A 2 2 93, 116, 154
Layman, W 1 2 529
Horton, L 2 2 359
Marshall, Early Jessup, 1 23 151
Marshall, Guy Jessup, 2 2 36
Marshall, Hugh Thompson, 1 2 137 2 1 266
Marshall, Joe (preacher) Jessup, 2 1 360
Marshall, Joel (Elder) Fain, C 1 2 184 1 1 183
Thomas, J 1 1 378
Marshall, Lane Jessup, 1 2 151
Marshall, Liza Thompson, 2 1 164
Marshall, Tyra Jessup, 2 1 70
Marshalls Lumber Company Fain C 1 1 262
Martin, Bennie Pendleton, B 1 1 192
Martin, Bonce Foddrell, P 1 1
Terry, N R 2 1 126
Carter, W C 2 1 135
Sayman 1 2 720
Martin, E T 1 1 312 1 2 474
Martin, Mrs. Bonce F. Martin, E T 1 1 77, 312 1 2 667, 872
Martin, Charlie Madison Martin, C M 1 2 580
Fulcher, R & G 1 2 77
Martin, Clarence M. Martin, C M 1 2 580 66

Carter, W C 1 2 628
Martin, Dr. Wood, G E 1 1 344
Martin, Ed Boaz 1 2 740
Martin, Ed (of Patrick Springs) Martin, C M 2 1 383 2 2 750
Carter, W C 1 1 269
Martin, Edna Alice (Clark) Clark, M F 1 1 120, 140
Martin, Elizabeth (Back) Terry, N R 2 1 126
Martin, E
Martin, George Martin, C M 1 2 580
Spangler, G 2 1 374
Martin, George (1st husband of Martin, Callie 1 1 127
Callie M. Ratliff Martin)
Martin, Harriet Fain, C 1 2 57
Martin, Jack Fulcher, R & E 1 2 320
Martin, Jerry Foddrell, P 1 1 298
Martin, (General) Joseph Hylton, B (US) 1 2 245
Martin, Luther (2nd husband of Martin, Callie 1 1 223
Callie Ratliff Martin)
Martin, Millie Wood, G E 1 1 223
Martin, (Dr.) Moir Fain, C 1 2 319
Martin, Noah Wood, R A 1 2 30
Martin, Dr. Richard S. Clark, M A 2 2 134
Thompson 2 1 455 2 2 24, 42
Clark, R L 1 2 175
Hall, P 1 2 176
Martin, Robert G. ("Bob") Martin, C M 1 1 49
Martin School Cruise, C 1 2 48 67
Martin, Troy Layman 1 2 664
Martin, Wesley Martin, C M 1 2 580 2 2 690
Martin, Willie Carter, W C 1 1 269
Martinsville Wood, G E 1 2 898
Martinsville Normal School Shelor, B 1 1 414
Martinsville Normal School 2 1 120
Thomas, J 1 2 454
Wood, G & C 1 2 100
Martinsville Clark, M A 2 2 35
Massie, Taylor Foddrell, P 1 1
Massie, Viola Martin, C M 2 1 52
Mayberry School Spangler, C 2 1 119
Mayberry Trading Post Wood, A 1 1 153
Mayberry, Virginia Harris, L 1 1 24, 28

Spangler, D O 1 1 22
Mays, Abe Clark, Ross 1 1 311
Mays, Ben Weaver, G 1 1 500
Thompson 1 1 422 3 2 154
Mays, Frank Spangler, C 3 2 382
Strock 2 1 190
Thompson 1 1 422
McAlexander, Eunice Y. McAlexander 1-2
McAlexander, Goldie M. H. Walker Church 1 1 157
McAlpine, Estelle Hopkins, E & B 5 2 23, 226
McCabe, Fred Penn, B 1 1 130
McCormick, Cora Hall, D 1 2 236
McDaniel, Bill Jessup 2 2 178 68
McKenzie, Charles Ellis McKenzie 5 1 56
McKenzie, Chester McKenzie
McKenzie, Erma (Mrs. Chester) McKenzie
Terry, N R 1 2 261
McKenzie, Louisa Rorrer McKenzie 5 1 56
McMillan, Croft Barnard, W 2 2 307
McPeak, Ed Hall, D 1 2 259
McPeak, Sam Hall, D 1 2 259
Meadows of Dan Shelor, J R 1 2 60
Spangler, C 2 2 39
Spangler, D O 1 2 133, 161
Meadows of Dan High School Shelor, J & C 2 1 237
Spangler, D O 1 1 83
Bolt, R 1 1 219
Shelor, B 2 1 228
Wood, A 1 1 230, 255
Meals East, G 2 1 124
Meat Wood, A 1 1 96
Medicine Houchins, M 1 1 217, 230
Slate, R & S 3 1 301
Methodists Clark, M A 1 2 90
Methuselah, Slate 5 1 52
Midwives Barbour, A 2 2 645
Bolt, R 1 2 268 3 2 184
Fain, C 1 2 57
Hall, D 1 2 110
Hopkins, B & E 4 2 54
Houchins, M 1 2 219

Penn, B 1 1 24
Pilson, A 1 2 281
Slate, R & S 2 1 385
Strock 1 1 79 69 2 1 22
Thomas, J 1 2 215
Wood, A 2 2 392, 414
Wood, G & C 1 1 400 2 1 20
Migrations Boaz, J 1 1 160
Kendrick, J 1 2 102, 240
Slate, R & S 3 22 236
Spangler, C 3 1 250, 298
Worley, L 1 1 316
Penn, B 1 2 85
Military Service Foddrell, M & T 1 1 304
Horton, L 1 1 377 2 1 81
Williams, D 1 2 67
Milking Kendrick, J 1 1 242
Miller, Grant McKenzie 2 1 202
Mills, Milling East, G 1 1 220
Mills, Milling, Gristmills Grady, E & L 1 1 29, 37 1 2 826
Hall, D 1 1 89
Hall, P 1 2 30, 81
Handy, J & N 1 1 430 1 2 20
Hopkins, B & E 2 1 257
Martin, C M 2 2 591, 600
Martin, L & C 1 1 44, 102
Slate, R & S 1 1 56
Spangler, C 2 2 241
Terry, N R 1 1 118
Handy, L 1 1 84
Layman, W 1 1 60, 100
Mills, Milling Kendrick, J 1 1 28, 82, 144 1 2 383
Mines, Mining, Women in Jessup, L 2 2 392
Ministers, Ministry Porter, P 1 1 27 1 2 206, 248
Mitchell, George Slate 4 2 380 70
Mitchell's Mill Slate, R & E 4 1 380
Moir, H.M. Clark, R L 1 2 264
Molasses East, G 1 1 492, 527
Fulcher, R & E 1 1 128
Hall, D 1 1 201
Kendrick, J 1 1 177

Pilson, O 2 2 754
Shelor, J & C 1 1 49, 64
Wood, G E 3 2 830, 872
Monroe, Bill Pendleton, B 1 1 303
Shelor, J R 1 2 1
Moore, Charlie Clark, R L 1 2 163
Moore, Georgia Plaster, J 1 2 81
Moore, James Edgar Wood, E M 1 1 35
Moore, Lula Ann Fulcher Wood, E M 1 1 39
Moore, Roody Foddrell, M & T 1 1 771
Moore, Rucher Layman 1 2 643
Moran, Blanco McKenzie 6 2 221
Morefield, Robert Jessup 1 2 236
Morris, Annie Carter, W C 1 2 535
Morris, Annie (Mrs. Noah) Weaver, G 1 1 520
Morris, Noah Weaver, G 1 1 520
Carter, W C 1 2 535
Morrison, (Patrick Springs Hotel) Wood, G E 1 1 120
Morrow, John (or Marr) Turner, J J 3 1 130
Moss, Noah Clark, M A 2 1 230
Mothers Home Hospital Clark, R L 1 2 175
East, G 2 2 733
Plaster, J 1 1 138, 185
Thompson, M E 2 1 455 71 2 2 24, 36
Mount Airy & Southern Railway, Barnard, W 1 1 186, 197, 402
Kibler Valley, Dinky 1 2 86 2 1 344, 358
Carter, W 1 1 343
Clark, R L 1 1 237
Strock 2 1 273
Mount Bethel School Clark, M E 1 1 39
(Carroll County)
Mountain Lions Barnard, W 2 1 255
Wood, A 1 1 125
Mountain People Williams, L 1 2 162
Mountains Hopkins, B & E 6 2 230-330
Movies, Silent, Theaters Clark, M A 1 2 223
Hopkins, W 1 2 118
Martin, E 1 1 92
Slate, R & S 4 2 362
Terry, N R 2 1 121
Hooker, J 1 2 139 2 1 20

Mules Kendrick, J 1 1 165
Murders Helms, A & E 1 2 15
Jessup, L 4 1 196
Weavers, G 1 1 50
Thompson, M E 2 2 190, 211
Music Barnard, W 1 2 233 3 1 289, 298
Bolt, R 3 1 190, 239
Foddrell, M & T 1 1 138, 360 1 2 26, 63, 273 2 1 2 6, 85 3 1 34-282 3 2 31 4 1 105
Foddrell, P 1 2 243
Inscore, W R 1 2 41
Kendrick, J 1 2 22
McAlexander, E 1 1 78, 107, 137, 166, 215, 264, 294, 300 72 1 2 59, 75, 123, 156
McKenzie, C & E 2 2 273
Pendleton, B 1 1 354, 368, 392 1 2 302, 328
Pilson, A 2 1 182
Shelor, J & C 2 1 20-345 2 2 48-255 3 1 1-190
Shelor, J R 1 1 162 1 2 1 2 1 167, 234 2 2 72
Shelor, W & A 1 1 125, 143, 154 1 2 48, 76
Strock 3 1 284-376 3 2 25
Williams, D 1 1 76-106, 179-407 1 2 308-453
Wood, G & C 1 1 270
Music/Religion Shelor, J & C 2 1 373
Rakes, O 2 2 22
Banjo Penn, B 1 1 169, 217
Music/Old Time Dancing Slate, R & S 4 1 120
Music/Singing Schools/Teaching Shelor, J & C 1 1 420 1 2 11 2 2 255
Music Shelor, W & A 1 2 373
Weaver, N 1 2 55
Williams 2 1 34
Music/Traditions Foddrell, M & T 1 1 30-181, 342 2 1 327
Patrick County HS 1 2 327
Musical Instruments Foddrell, M & T 2 1 60
McAlexander, E 1 2 36
Pendleton, B 1 2 109, 121, 134, 142
Shelor, W & A 1 2 35
Williams, D 1 1 34-76, 106-176 1 2 77, 107, 116, 200, 280
Musicians Cruise, C 1 2 117
Hall, D 1 2 236, 259 73
Handy, J & N 1 2 178

Harbour, K 1 2 818
Weaver, N 1 2 30
Names East, G 2 1 385
Nance, Bob Carter, W C 1 1 269
National Recovery Administration Plaster, L 1 1 45
National Youth Administration Pilson, O 2 1 58, 180, 200
Clark, L L 1 1 159
Neal, Ed Clark, M A 2 1 35
Neighbors Barnard, W 3 1 324
Clark, M A 1 2 100
Culler, C 1 1 76, 91 1 2 44
East, G 1 1 143, 345
Foley, R 1 2 74
Handy, J & N 1 2 295, 337
Harris, L 2 1 33
Houchins, M 3 1 158
Howell, R 1 1 32
Hylton, B 1 2 90
Nelson, David Terry, N R 2 2 211
Nettle Ridge School Grady, F & L 1 1 91 1 2 477, 562, 580
New Deal Programs Spangler, D O 2 1 181
New Year's Day Thompson, M E 3 1 313
Newberg, Van A. Spangler, C 3 1 215
Newcomers Hylton, B 1 2 134
Kendrick, J 1 2 310
Rakes, O 1 1 46, 171
Slate, R & S 1 2 203
Thomas, J 1 1 425 1 2 30
Neighbors Williams, V 1 1 68
Wood, A 2 2 74, 362
Worley, L 1 1 134 74
Newcomers Barnard, J 1 1 360
Boaz, J 1 2 498, 512
Bolt, R 2 1 87
Clark, L L 1 2 346
Clark, M A 2 3 321
Culler, C 1 2 257
Edwards, M 1 1 403
Fulcher, R & E 2 2 33
Hardin Reynolds E S 1 2 147
Helms, A & E 1 2 36

Hopkins, B & E 3 2 325
Hopkins, L 1 1 233, 292, 346
Horton, L 3 1 105
Patrick County HS 1 2 115
Stuart E S 1 2 245
Terry, N R 2 2 344, 421
Williams, V 1 2 590
Newman, George Carter, W C 1 1 264
Newman, Ham Hopkins, E & B 1 1 88
Newman, Jim Hopkins, E & B 1 1 88
Newspapers East, G 2 1 344
Slate, R & S 2 1 78
Boaz 1 1 50, 605
Nickleson Handy, L S 1 1 84
Nicknames Weaver, N 1 2 590
No Business Mountain Plaster, J 1 1 374
Wood, G E 3 2 636
Nolen Family Rakes O 1 2 117, 200
Nolen, Posey (Preacher) Foley, R E 1 2 141, 162
Nowlin, Arch Carter, W C 1 2 628
Nowlin, Tom Martin, C M 1 2 546
Carter, W C 1 2 628
Nowlin, Walter Martin, C M 1 2 546
Nurses, Nursing East, G 2 2 747 75
Hall, P 1 1 203,k 369, 429
Harris, H 1 1 74, 100, 104, 350, 373 1 2 514
Nursing Homes Barnard, W 3 1 340
Slate, R & S 2 1 133
Thompson, M E 3 2 216
Williams, D 3 2 148, 154, 162
Occupations Pilson, H 1 1 259
Ogburn, Alva McKenzie 6 2 211
Oliver, Queenie Barbour, A 2 2 645
Omahundo, Melvin Spangler, C 1 1 314
Orchards Clark, R L 1 1 189
Fulcher, R E 1 2 112
Hopkins, B & E 1 1 134
Martin, E 1 2 571
Plaster, L 1 1 92
Terry, N R 1 1 286, 293
Williams, D 2 1 347

Williams, W 1 2 553, 564, 606, 646
McKenzie, C & E 5 1 320
Martin, L & C 1 2 184, 196
Ore, Charlie Carter, W 2 1 165
Outsiders Williams, L 3 2 71
Ozarks Williams, L 1 2 129
Pace of Life Penn, B 1 2 260
Pack, Isom Clifton, E N 1 1 137
Packett, Paola Inscore 2 2 74
Parent-Teacher Association Wood E M 1 2 509-550
Parks, Recreation Turner, E M 1 1 440 1 2 21, 44, 75
Kibler Valley Barnard, W 3 1 215
Patrick Central School Hylton, A H 1 1 35 76 1 2 1, 12, 20, 35
Terry, N R 2 2 33
Turner, E M 2 2 170, 315, 340, 415
Patrick County Attractions Harbour, K 1 2 791
Patrick County HS 1 1 24
Roberson, W 1 1 337
Worley, L 1 2 557
Beauty Williams, L 3 2 55
Patrick County Board of Turner, E M 2 1 430
Supervisors 2 2 22
Patrick County Changes Barnard, J 1 1 65
Boaz, J 1 1 85
Clark, M A 1 2 390
Foddrell, M & T 1 2 150
Hall, P 1 1 247 1 2 357
Handy, J & W 1 1 85, 103
Harris, L 1 2 180, 226
Hopkins, L 1 1 339
Hopkins, W 2 2 158
Howell, R 1 2 29
Hylton, B 1 1 342
Plaster, J 1 2 385, 415
Rakes, O 1 1 186
Roberson, W 1 1 156
Spangler, D O 1 1 369, 397
Terry, M S 2 2 21
Terry, N R 3 1 28
Williams, V 1 1 96
Wood, R A 1 1 149

Worley, L 1 1 160, 169
Patrick County Character Clark, M F 3 2 98, 120
of People
Patrick County Court House Hooker, J 1 1 405, 429
Patrick County Emigrants Pilson, O 4 2 795
Patrick County Emigration East, G 1 2 895 2 1 24
Patrick County Employment McKenzie, C & E 2 2 73
Patrick County Fair Shelor, J R 2 1 425 2 2 1 77
Patrick County Famous Families Hylton, B 1 2 245, 293
Patrick County Future Clark, L L 1 2 20
Hardin Reynolds E S 1 2 210
Hopkins, W 2 2 300, 400
Patrick County HS 1 1 260 1 2 196
Pilson, H 1 1 145
Stuart E S 1 1 276, 425
Turner, E M 2 1 52
Patrick County Government Barnard, W 1 2 212
Culler, C 1 2 270
Patrick County Historic Museum Boaz, J 1 2 740
Clark, L L 1 2 410
Patrick County History Bolt, R 2 1 240, 255
Turner, E M 1 2 420 2 1 20 2 2 180
Patrick County Jail Clark, M F 2 1 65, 85, 105
Hooker, J 1 1 437
Patrick County Library Boaz, J 1 2 740
Clark, L L 1 1 1 2
Patrick County Mountains Handy, J & N 2 2 420
Patrick Co Orchard Company Wood, G E 1 2 535
Patrick County Pride in Hopkins, L 1 1 76
Patrick County Problems Patrick County HS 1 1 90
Stuart E S 1 2 23
Patrick County Progress Clark, M F 1 1 360, 380
Turner, E M 1 1 47, 60
Patrick County Project Clark, M F 3 2 140
Hylton, B 1 2 328
Porter, P 2 2 409
Roberson, W 1 2 333
Sate, R & S 5 1 42 78
Turner, E M 2 2 130
Weaver, G 1 1 310
Patrick County Quality of Life Porter, P 2 2 258

Stuart E S 1 1 24

Weaver, L 1 1 235

Patrick County "Rag" Williams, L 3 2 35

Foddrell, M & T 2 1 104

Patrick County Reapportionment Terry, M S 1 1 261

Patrick County Representation in Terry, M S 1 1 190, 251

General Assembly 2 1 261

Patrick County Residents Spangler, D O 1 2 372

Character Turner, E M 1 1 266

Patrick County, Returning to Hopkins, L 1 1 124, 170

Patrick County Scenery Clark, R L 1 2 22

Patrick County Settlers Spangler, C 1 1 63, 111 1 2 30, 95

Patrick County Transfer Company Plaster, L 1 2 479

Patrick Springs East, G 1 1 32, 45, 57 1 2 643, 666

Fulcher, R E 1 2 167

Layman, W 1 1 40, 438 1 2 498

Martin, C M 2 1 89, 91

Plaster, J 1 2 168, 215, 281

Patrick Springs Bottling Company Layman, W 1 1 115-150

Patrick Springs Hotel Clark, J M 4 1 56

East, G 1 1 150, 179, 194

Plaster, J 1 1 223, 264

Wood, G E 1 1 82, 85, 95, 120, 130, 160, 185, 198, 206, 217, 258, 281

Layman, W 1 1 366 79

Patriotism Boaz, J 1 2 605

Patterson, Miss Harris, H P 1 2 514

Patton, (Gen.) George Slate 4 1 80 on tape catalog

Peach Seeds Plaster, L 1 1 135

Pedigo, Mac Barnard, W 3 1 65

Pendleton, Babe Wood, G & C 1 1 120

Pendleton, Buddy Pendleton, B

Pendleton, Calvin Pendleton, B 1 1 137

Pendleton, Elva Pendleton, B 1 1 100

Pendleton, Garvis Pendleton, B 1 1 209

Pendleton, Lonnie Lane Pendleton, B 1 1 192

Pendleton School Foley, R 1 1 45

Penn, Guthrie ("Gert") Barber 1 1 191

Perdue, Harry Carter, W C 1 1 269

Perkins Hotel Hooker, J 1 1 134

Weavers, G 1 1 550

Perry Business College - Shelor, J R 1 2 44

Martinsville
Philadelphia Foddrell, M & T 3 1 325
Phillips, Harry Williams, L 1 2 60
Phlegar, Charlie Spangler, C 4 1 247
Philpott, A.L. Clark, M F 3 1 295, 365
Terry, M S 1 1 79
Photography Jessup, L 1 1 370
Turner, J J 3 1 325
Martin, L & C 1 2 647
Pilson, Alpha Ella (Morrison) Pilson, A 1-2 80
Pilson, "Blondie" Woodrow Pilson, A 1 1 405
Turner, J J 1 2 620
Pilson, Carrie McKenzie 5 2 215
Pilson, Elizabeth Spangler, D O 1 1 181
Pilson Family Pilson, O 4 2 795
Pilson, Herbert Terry, M S 1 2 107
Pilson, Howard Clark, M F 3 1 125
Pilson, Ophus Eugene ("O.E.") Pilson, O E 4
Pilson, Samuel ("Squire") Hooker, J 2 1 184
Pilson, Will Pilson, A 1 1 156
Pine Tree School Terry, N R 1 2 184
Pinnacles Dam Project Barnard, W 1 2 65, 79 2 1 39
Bolt, R 1 1 211
Carter, W 2 1 243
Jessup, L 4 1 287, 345
Plaster, L 1 1 162
Shelor, J & C 4 1 25
Slate, R & S 2 1 166, 199
Thomas, J 1 2 312
Spangler, C 2 2 91, 113, 134
Williams, D 2 1 107
Pinnacles of Dan Spangler, C 1 1 90
Pinnacle View School Jessup, L 1 2 207
Plantations Spangler, C 3 1 241
Planting (by signs) Houchins, M 4 2 338
Slate, R & S 4 2 133
Williams D 3 1 134, 150
Plaster, Darrell Martin, Callie 1 2 674
Plaster, Donald Martin, Callie 1 2 674
Martin, C M (Clarence) 2 1 146 81
Plaster, George East, Gladys 2 2 784

Martin, C M 1 1 115, 150
Shelor, W & A 1 1 397 1 2 1
Plaster, Pauline Wood, E M 1 1 193
Pneumonia Handy, L 1 1 325
Poisons Shelor, J & C 2 1 439 2 2 11
Politics Clark, M F 3 1 76, 87, 120, 131, 150
Barnard, W 3 1 126, 135, 144
Clark, J M 2 2 321
Clark, R L 1 2 386
Hooker, J 3 1 14-205
Horton, L 2 2 188
Slate, R & SW 2 2 377
Weaver, N 1 1 525
Wood, G & C 1 2 350
Clark, M F 1 1 302, 310, 346 2 2 10 3 1 155, 178, 185, 202
Spangler, D O 2 1 268, 272
Turner, E M 2 2 240
Poole, Charlie Pendleton, B 1 1 84
Poor Mans Beer Spangler, D O 2 1 127
Popcorn Martin, C M 3 2 600
Population Inscore, W R 1 1 280 2 2 149
Hylton, B 1 1 106, 153
Culler, C 1 1 258
Pilson, H 1 1 280
Horton, L 2 2 120
Plaster, J 1 2 168
Turner, E M 1 1 71
Porches, Porticos Slate, R & S 3 1 104
Post Offices Clark, M A 2 2 177
Layman, W 1 1 80, 90 82
Rakes, O 1 1 17 1 2 2
Shelor, B 2 2 147
Thomas, J 1 2 323
Claudville Martin, E 1 1 177
Critz 1 2 743
Worley, L 1 1 32
Elamsville Culler, C 1 2 76
The Hollow Hopkins, B & E 1 1 413
Howells Barnard, W 2 2 332
Kibler East, G 1 1 109
Patrick Springs Hooker, J 1 2 24

Stuart Thompson, M E 1 2 177
Pot Racks Slate, R & S 1 1 34
Poverty Horton, L 1 2 235
Powell, Al Thompson 1 2 147
Powell, Aleck Thompson 2 2 319
Powell, Charles Foddrell, P 1 2 150
Slate 3 1 174
Powell, Jean Thompson 2 2 319
Powell School Strock 1 1 262
Powell's Lumber Company Fain, C 1 1 262
Prayer Meetings Shelor, J R 2 2 223
Houchins, M 4 2 410
Preachers Houchins, M 3 1 89
Mitchell, I 1 1 342 1 3 235
Strock 2 1 389 2 2 88 3 2 199
Williams, L 1 1 246
Weaver, G 1 1 95, 113
Wood, G E 2 1 145
Presbyterian Ministry Williams, L 1 2 153
Price, (Governor) Hooker, J 2 2 20 83
Prillaman, Perry Carter, W C 2 1 37
Primat Lumber Corporation Barnard, W 3 1 377
Williams, D 3 1 248, 266
Primitive Baptist Association Barbour, A 2 1 445
Meetings Fain, C 1 1 172
Hylton, A H 1 2 95
Barnard, W 1 1 173 1 2 270, 278, 286 2 2 240 3 1 75
Clark, M A 1 2 90
Foddrell, M & T 3 2 280
McKenzie 2 1 445 2 2 22, 28
Jail Clark, M F 2 1 90, 105
Primitive Baptist Meetings Roberson, W 1 1 196
Thompson, M E 2 1 277, 297
Rakes, O 1 2 189 2 1 147
Primitive Baptist Meetings Shelor, J & C 2 1 373
Worley, L 1 2 704
Private Enterprise Hylton, B 1 1 235
Professions Clark, M F 1 1 95 1 2 320
Prohibition Clark, J M 4 2 100
Bootlegging Spangler, D O 2 1 127
Providence United Methodist Martin, C M 2 1 104

Church Wood, E M 1 1 35 1 2 580
Public Works Administration Handy, J & N 1 1 341
Puckett, Jimmy Hopkins, E & B 4 2 88
Puckett, Raleigh Pendleton, B 1 1 84
Purcell, Wayne D. Terry, N R 2 2 180
Purdy (or Purney), Andrew Barber 1 1 430
Quality of Life Barbour, A 2 2 890
Barnard, J 1 1 199 84
Foddrell, M & T 1 2 242
Foddrell, P 1 2 88
Hardin Reynolds E S 1 1 27
Inscore, W R 1 1 425, 452
Pilson, A 2 2 45
Shelor, J R 1 2 122
Weaver, N 1 2 410, 470, 510
Quesenberry, Mallie Jessup 2 1 311
Quesenberry, Tyler Bolt 3 2 311
Jessup 1 1 370
Quilting Barnard, W 1 1 321
Boaz, J 1 1 136
Cruise, C 1 2 292 2 1 27
Fulcher, R & E 1 2 407 2 1 35
Hopkins, B & E 7 1 203
Inscore, W R 1 2 209
Layman, W 1 2 884
Mary Horner Walker Church 1 1 1 2
New Hope Church 1 1 1 2
Quilting Pilson, A 1 1 280
Slate, R & S 3 1 340
Strock 3 1 181, 207
Williams, L 2 1 223
Williams, N 1 2 199
Rabbit Gums Pilson, A 2 2 61
Race Relations Foddrell, P 1 2 100, 300
Houchins, M 1 2 354 2 1 262
Penn, B 1 1 57
Radcliff, Green Worley, L 1 1 32
Radford College Worley, L 1 1 382, 443
Strock 3 2 119, 135
Radio Programs, Radios Barbour, A 2 2 495
Barnard, W 3 2 251, 267

Culler, C 1 2 153
East, G 2 1 172 85
Foley, R 1 2 59
Handy, J & N 2 2 260-327
Harris, O 1 2 788
Helms, A & E 1 2 52
Hooker, J 2 2 400
Hopkins, B & E 3 2 247
Howell, R 1 2 68
Hylton, B 1 1 400
Inscore, W R 2 2 317
East, G 1 2 219
McAlexander, E 1 1 294 1 2 123
Pilson, O 1 2 535
Spangler, C 4 2 193, 216
Spangler, D O 2 2 362
Terry, N R 2 1 116
Williams, V 1 2 520
Wood, A 1 2 417
Wood, G & C 2 1 400
Worley, L 1 2 512
Thomas, J 1 2 200, 244
Pilson, A 2 1 347
Ragsdale, Fritz Carter, W C 1 1 269
Plaster, J 1 1 138
Rail Service Kendrick, J 1 1 443
Railroad, Ties, Narrow Gauge Martin, C M 1 1 183, 350 2 1 310, 336 3 1 105
Railroad, Ties, Narrow Gauge Clifton, B 1 1 330
Fain, C 1 2 271
Turner, J J 3 1 395 3 2 607
Wood, G E 1 2 749, 782, 791, 822
Pilson, O 1 1 445 1 2 486
Martin, C M 1 1 170, 176, 213
Narrow Gauge 3 1 63, 141, 161
Weaver, B 1 2 550
Hopkins, W 1 1 88
Railway Express Carter, W 2 2 622
Rakes, Ovilla Sue Rakes, O 1-2
Rakes, Raft Barnard, W 1 1 209 86
Rationing, WWII Spangler, D O 1 1 373, 422, 447, 453

Ratliff, Harrison East, Gladys 2 2 859
Ray, (or Wray), Jess Carter, W C 1 1 269
RJ Reynolds Memorial Hospital Harris, O 1 2 733
Reading Spangler, D O 2 2 200
Thompson, M E 1 2 159
Turner, J J 3 2 832
Recreation Clark, M A 1 2 180, 223
Foley, R 1 2 325
Hall, P 1 1 388
Harris, L 1 2 35
Helms, A & E 1 1 86
Horton, L 2 2 33, 102
Shelor, B 1 1 288 2 1 87
Strock 1 1 260 3 1 273, 284
Weaver, G 1 1 260
Weaver, N 1 1 150
Inscore, W R 2 2 353, 376
Games Williams, W 1 1 201
Hardin Reynolds E S 1 1 157, 343
Barnard, J 1 1 265
Clark, M F 2 2 106, 230
Recreation Dept Pilson, O 2 2 840
Sports Wood, A 1 2 103
Sports 2 2 50
Youth Patrick County HS 1 1 96, 425 1 2 22
Red Bank Church Barnard, W 1 1 123
Horton, L 1 2 197 2 2 274
Red Cross Barnard, W 2 1 411
Jessup, L 4 1 58
Redistricting Clark, M F 3 1 355
Refrigerators Grady, F & L 1 1 301
Inscore, W R 2 1 425 2 2 42 87
Thompson, M E 2 1 89
Wood, G E 2 1 78
Religion Clark, M A 1 2 49, 70, 90
Clark, M F 3 2 5, 20, 30, 43
Fulcher, A W 1 2 63
Hal, P 1 2 417
Hooker, J 1 2 226
Horton, L 2 2 44-101
Hylton, A H 1 2 82

Patrick County HS 1 2 399
Pilson, A 2 1 90
Pilson, O 3 1 300, 345
Strock 2 2 153, 336-3 1 143-181 3 1 357
Weaver, N 1 2 435
Renmark, Carol Terry, N R 1 1 257
Renmark, Ronnie Terry, N R 1 1 257
Restaurants Weaver, G 1 1 520
Restorations- Historic Stuart E S 1 1 342
Retirement Clark, J M 4 2 198
Cox, W 2 2 780
Cruise, C 1 2 265
Wood, E M 1 2 708
Revenuers, Distilling, Illicit Spangler, C 3 2 137, 145, 382-
Liquor 4 1 20-290, 377-4 2 23-82
Revivals Mitchell, I 1 1 311
Pilson, A 1 2 66, 80
Weaver, G 1 1 407
Revolutionary War Bolt, R 2 1 290
Reynolds, Annie Terry, N R 1 2 201
Reynolds, Calloway Wood, A 1 1 15, 58
Reynolds, Claude Clar, M A 2 1 35
Reynolds, Gerald Shelor, W & A 1 1 197 88
Reynolds, Hardin Spangler, C 3 1 241
Harris, H P 1 1 122
Reynolds Homestead Boaz, J 1 2 867
Clark, R L 1 2 22
Slate, R & S 4 2 411
Terry, M S 3 1 428
Turner, E M 2 2 130
Weaver, G 1 1 310
Weaver, N 1 2 480
Reynolds, Ida Barbour, A L 1 2 803
Reynolds, James Wood, A 1 1 15
Reynolds, James Benton Bolt 3 2 113
Reynolds, Jesse Ben Terry, N R 2 2 401
Reynolds, J.F. Pilson, O E 1 1 420
Reynolds, J. Sargeant Terry, M S 3 1 326, 392
Reynolds, Lynn Bolt 3 1 400
Reynolds, Nancy Terry, N R 1 2 201
Terry, M S 3 1 428

Reynolds, Oliver Helms 1 2 15
Reynolds, P.C. Wood, A 1 1 15
Reynolds, R.J. (Richard Joshua) Terry, N R 1 2 151
Hopkins, E & B 2 1 56
Reynolds, Samson Terry, N R 2 2 401
Reynolds, T. Faye Thompson 1 1 268
Reynolds, Will Terry, N R 1 2 151
Rich Bent/ Busted Rock Clifton, F 1 2 228
Richardson, J. Mason Pilson, A 1 2 35
Richardson, Larry Pendleton, B 1 1 273 89
Richardson, Robert East, Gladys 2 2 284
Ring Jailing for Apples Martin, L & C 1 1 196
Roads Barnard ,W 1 2 378
Bolt, R 1 1 143, 160
Clark, M A 1 1 18, 213
Culler, C 1 1 205, 230
East, G 1 1 171 2 1 152
Fain, C 1 1 365
Grady, F & L 1 2 504, 526
Hardin Reynolds E S 1 1 343
Harris, O 1 1 151
Hooker, J 1 1 165, 190
Hopkins, B & E 1 2 93 2 1 35
Hylton, B 1 1 245
Inscore, W R 1 1 262 1 2 263
Kendrick, J 1 2 422
McAlexander, E 2 1 164
Martin, C M 2 2 573
Rakes, O 1 1 53
Shelor, J R 1 1 78
Terry, N R 3 1 28
Williams, D 3 1 32
Wood, G & C 1 2 20
Wood, G E 3 1 228, 264, 280, 329, 344, 369
Worley, L 1 1 341
Clark, J M 1 1 114
Condition Turner, J J 3 2 585
Handy, L 1 1 210, 212
Wood, R A 1 2 53
Construction Helms, A & E 1 1 60, 216, 243
Clifton, F 1 1 400

History 1 2 134, 181
Edwards, M 1 1 181
Foley, R 1 1 83
Harbour, K 1 1 298 1 2 584, 590
Hopkins, L 1 1 246
Hopkins, W 2 1 64, 302
Williams, V 1 1 280, 345
Boaz, J 1 1 183
Roads Plaster J 1 2 117
Plaster, L 1 2 620 90
Roberson, W 1 1 156
Macadam Slate, R & S 1 1 149
T Spangler, C 1 1 63, 90
US 58 Clark, R L 1 1 50
Roberson (or Robertson), Charlie Martin, C M 1 1 190
Roberson, Henry Worley, L 1 1 32
Roberson, Lardon Thomas, J 1 2 323
Roberson, Roy Worley, L 1 1 22
Roberson, Winifred C. Roberson, W C 1
Robertson, Abe Pilson, A 2 2 98
Robertson, Charlie Barnard, W 1 1 402
Fain, C 1 2 184
Robertson, Uria Martin, Callie 1 2 647
Robinson, Cave Wood, A 2 2 414
Rock Houses Wood, R A 1 2 53
Rock Quarries Hooker, J 1 1 208-252
Rock Spring (Critz) Martin, E 1 2 743, 770
Rodgers, Hoyt Plaster, J 1 1 138
Rodgers, Jimmy Foddrell, M & T 3 1 120
Rodgers, Mrs. William Foddrell, P 1 2 200
Roosevelt F D Spangler, D O 2 1 240
Rorrer, David Hopkins, E & B 6 2 23
McKenzie 2 1 336
Rorrer, Gladys Fain, C 1 1 70
Rorrer, James Tyler Hopkins, E & B 6 1 443
Rorrer, Lucinda Williams Hopkins, E & B 6 1 443 6 2 23 91
Rorrer, Mike Hopkins, E & B 6 2 23
Rorrer, Oregon Jessup 1 2 137 2 1 192
Rorrer, Thomas McKenzie 2 1 337 5 1 44
Rorrer, Tottsie Fulcher, J & N 1 2 295
Ross, Bell Turner, J J 1 2 620

Ross, Chris Turner, J J 1 2 620
Ross, Hulda Thompson 3 2 417
Ross, Kitty Hopkins, E & B 2 1 366
Ross Patty Pilson, O E 1 1 237
Ross School Pilson, O 1 1 199
Rotary Club Thompson, M E 2 2 89
Rucker, Fred Thompson 1 2 51
Rucker, Lark Thompson 2 2 400
Rug Braiding Williams, L 2 1 54
"Rugged Individualism" Thompson' M E 1 2 222
Rye Cove School Fain, C 1 1 33, 97
Salesmen Clark, J M 1 1 167 2 1 382
Saloons Wood, G E 2 2 561
Sanhedrin Kerry, M S 4 1 114
Sawmills, Sawmilling, logging
Barbour, A 1 1 58, 167, 210, 394 1 2 487,515,554,560,610
Barnard, W 2 1 358, 391
Clark, R L 1 1 227, 253 92
Clifton, F 1 1 149
Edwards, M 1 1 167
Foddrell, M & T 1 1 199, 254
Sawmills Hall, D 1 1 281
Harbour, K 1 2 549
Harris, O 1 1 439
Helms, A & E 1 1 118
Jessup, L 1 2 289
Kendrick, J 1 2 121
Slate, R & S 3 1 161 4 1 30, 40
Williams, V 1 1 106 1 2 640
Scales, Aif Hall, D 1 1 281
School Board Elections Clark, M F 3 1 389
Horton, L 2 2 349
School Breakings Jessup, L 1 2 74, 137
School Budgets Clark, M F 2 1 3 2 2 300, 317
School Buildings Harris, L 1 1 206
School Buses Terry, N R 2 2 68
School Consolidation Barnard, J 1 1 228
Bolt, R 2 1 105
Clark, R L 1 1 78
Fulcher, R & E 2 2 105, 137
Harris, L 2 2 56

Harris, O 1 2 691
Hooker, J 1 1 81
Hopkins, W 2 2 183
Horton, L 1 2 188 93
Inscore, W R 1 1 130
McKenzie, C & E 4 1 335
Shelor, J R 1 2 182
Slate, R & S 1 1 139
Spangler, D O 1 1 145,184,291,315,369
Strock 1 2 417
Terry, N R 2 1 160
Weaver, G 1 1 256
Wood, A 1 1 253
Worley, L 1 2 638
School Discipline Clark, M F 2 2 370 3 1 8
Cruise, C 1 1 219
Fain, C 1 1 87
Foley, R 1 1 52, 157
McKenzie, C & E 4 1 32
Patrick County HS 2 1 43
Pilson, O 2 2 555, 630
Spangler, C 2 1 128, 155, 167, 185
Spangler, D O 1 2 21, 26, 321
Strock 1 1 288 3 2 67
Thomas, J 1 1 229
Thompson, M E 3 2 234, 267
Wood, E M 1 1 385
School Integration Terry, M S 2 2 57 2 1 320, 343
Spangler, D O 1 1 369
School Prayer Hopkins, W 2 2 237
School Sports Pilson, O 2 2 840
School Transportation Clark, M F 1 1 39, 50
Schools Barnard, W 1 1 128, 136, 144
Bolt, R 1 1 63, 111
Clark, M A 1 1 134
Fain, C 1 1 97
Grady, F & L 1 1 61, 77, 91, 101 1 2 477, 491, 500, 530
Hooker, J 1 1 42
Howell, R 1 1 181
Hylton, A H 1 1 370 1 2 1
Inscore, W R 1 2 270 94 2 2 63

Martin, E 1 1 421 1 2 468
Martin, L & C 1 2 663
Mitchell, I 1 2 390-448
Patrick County HS 1 1 295, 324
Plaster, J 1 2 7, 81
Rakes, O 1 2 100
Slate, R & S 1 1 88
Spangler, C 2 1 260
Thompson, M E 1 1 94
Wood, A 1 1 353, 405
Wood, E M 1 1 96
School-American Vs. European Porter, P 1 2 67
School-Anecdotes Spangler, C 2 1 409
Weaver, N 1 1 590
School-Changes In Clark, M A 1 1 171
Schools-Changes in Curriculum McKenzie, C & E 4 1 292
School-Community Fulcher, R & E 2 2 79
School-Compulsory Attendance Pilson, O 2 1 370
School-Corn Crib Strock 1 1 100, 115
School-Federal Programs McKenzie, C & E 4 2 23
School-Funding Pilson, O 1 2 850 2 1 414, 437
Terry, N R 2 2 68 2 2 108
School-Funding Pilson, O 1 2 850 2 1 414, 437
Terry, N R 2 2 68 2 2 108
School-Funding, Shortages Weaver, G 1 1 185, 200
School-History Fulcher, A W 1 1 43-101
Fulcher, R & E 2 1 122, 137
Harris, L 1 1 173, 198, 227 2 1 370
Shelor, B 1 1 350 95 1 2 23, 35 2 1 24
Thomas, J 1 1 198
Weaver, N 1 1 608, 625 1 2 3
Wood, G & C 2 1 50
Schools in Early Patrick County Pilson, O 1 1 185
Schools-One Room Clark, R L 1 1 78
Clifton, F 1 1 110, 210
Cruise, C 1 1 151
East, G 1 1 236
Foley, R 1 1 45
Hall, D 1 1 44
Hopkins, B & E 1 1 328
Strock 1 1 238-278 1 2 258-305, 417

Schools Turner, E M 2 2 85
Wood, G E 2 1 116, 164 2 2 815, 864
Wood, R A 1 1 186
School-Pranks Shelor, J R 2 1 24
School-Small vs Large Terry, M S 1 1 383
School-Two Room McAlexander, E 2 2 282
School-Woolwine Weaver, N 1 1 133
Scott, Bob Houchins 1 2 101
Scott, Ceph Jessup 1 2 446
Scott, Donald Scott, Donald
Scott, Granville Boston Spangler, C 1 2 203
Scott, J. Hugh Spangler, C 1 1 20
Scott, S.C. Wood, A
Scott, Simon Wood, G & C 1 1 90
Wood, A 2 1 112 1 1 313
Harris, L B 1 1 349
Barnard, W 1 2 146 96 2 2 30
Shelor, B 1 1 177
Scott, Webster Clifton, F 1 1 110
Scott, (Senator) William Pilson, O E 3 2 507
Scruggs, Earl Shelor, J R 1 2
Sectionalism Patrick County HS 1 1 350
Weaver, G 1 1 235, 280
Segregation Foddrell, M & T 1 2 150 3 1 347
Penn, B 1 1 24
Self-Sufficiency Boaz, J 1 1 136
Clark, R 1 2 270, 406
Hall, P 1 2 81
Handy, J & N 1 1 415
Helms, A & E 1 1 154
Horton, L 1 2 66
Self-Sufficiency Hylton, B 1 1 176
Martin, C M 2 1 345
Roberson, W 1 2 30
Thompson, M E 2 1 99
Wood, R A 1 1 232, 245, 308
Worley, L 1 1 382
Senior Citizen's Groups Williams, L 2 2 274
Sewing Cruise, C 1 1 312, 322
Fulcher, A W 1 1 285
Sex Education Hopkins, W 2 2 250

Shady Grove Church Martin, C M 2 1 104
Shamblin School Hopkins, B & E 2 1 366-433
Hopkins, W 1 1 35
McKenzie, C & E 5 2 127
Shappes, Cecil McAlexander 1 1 78, 370
Sheep Raising Hylton, B 1 1 176
McKenzie, C & E 5 2 83
Wood, R A 1 2 247 97
Shelbourne, Dr. Terry, N R 2 1 70
Shelor, Babe Bolt 1 2 54
Shelor, Bertie (Marshall) Shelor, B 1- 2
Shelor, Cozier Harris, L B 3 1 159, 207
Shelor, Dula Harris, L B 1 1 173
Shelor, Ella Harris, L B 1 1 173
Shelor, Eloise Shelor, J R 2 2 110
Shelor, Elroy Shelor, B 1 1 21
Shelor, Frank Shelor, J R 1 2 357, 393
Shelor, J & C 1 2 420
Shelor, George Jessup 3 1 67
Shelor, Hannah Hall, D 1 1 36
Shelor, Jessee & Clarice Shelor, J & C 1-4
Shelor, John Bolt 2 1 207
Shelor, Judge Bolt 3 2 226
Shelor, Lester Bolt 3 2 113
Shelor, Lilla Strock 2 1 141
Shelor, Paul Shelor, J R 2 2 390
Shelor, Pierre Shelor, J R 2 1 191
Sheppard, Weaver, G 1 1 940
Sheppard, Charles Terry, N R 1 2 404
Shingle Shops Hall, D 1 2 447
Shockley, Noan (Prof.) Thompson 1 1 179
Shoes Hall, D 1 2 383
Handy, J & N 3 2 70
Handy, L 1 1 181 98
Homemade Wood, R A 1 1 245
Shoemaking Barnard, W 2 2 30
Harbour, K 1 1 402
Harris, L 1 1 349
Hopkins, B & E 1 2 360
Repair Hopkins, B & E 1 2 349
Horton, L 2 1 272

Martin, C M 3 1 300
Wood, A 1 1 282, 313, 353
"Shootin" Creek Kendrick, J 1 2 52, 64
Short, Bob Slate 4 1 40
Shough Mill Martin, C M 2 2 591
Shough, (Rev.) Jacob Plaster, J 1 1 51
Shrouds Fulcher, A W 1 2 29
Shuff, Virginia Plaster, J 1 1 35
Patrick Springs Fulcher, A W 1 2 80
Sickness Handy, L 1 1 325
Silver Mines Barnard, W 1 1 209
Bolt, R 2 1 273
Simmons, Alpha Thompson 1 1 230
Simmons, Charlie (preacher) Jessup 3 2 92
Simmons, Edgar Hardy, J & N 3 2 210
Simmons, Rawleigh Jessup 4 1 116
Singing Schools Cruise, C 1 1 135
Slate, Samuel and Sally Slate 5 tapes
Slaves, Slavery Barnard, W 1 1 64, 82, 336, 356
Clifton, F 1 1 67
Harris, L 3 1 34, 258
Houchins, M 2 1 328 3 1 351 4 1 192
Hylton, A H 1 1 170 99
Penn, B 1 2 368
Small, Laura Belle Hylton, A 1 1 420
Small Pox Boaz, J 1 2 453
Hopkins, B & E 7 1 400
Wood, A 1 2 279, 300, 326
Smart, Cindy (Mrs. George) Thomas, J 1 2 215
Smart, Donnie Pilson, A 1 1 119
Smith, Arnold Bolt 1 2 392
Smith, Herbert McKenzie, C & E 1 2 134, 147
Smith, Lena Shelor, J R 1 1 24
Smith, Monk Spangler, C 3 1 215
Smith, Newton Hopkins, E & B 2 2 295
Strock 1 2 318
Smith, Plummer Strock 1 2 50, 318
2 2 398
Smith River Church Hopkins, L 1 2 486
Smith, Roy (Rev.) Strock 1 2 50, 318 2 2 398
Smith, Thomas Shelor, J R 1 1 125

Smith, Virginia Henderson McKenzie, C & E 1 2 134, 147
Smith, Watt Smith, J J 1 2 675
Smoking Tobacco Slate, R & S 3 2 207
Snakes- Antidotes Handy, J & N 2 2 56
Spangler, C 2 2 410, 445
Snow, Snowstorms Edwards, M 1 1 429
Wood, G E 3 1 434 3 2 496, 590
1911 Bolt, R 1 1 111, 135
Soap Making Boaz, J 1 1 136 100
Edwards, M 1 1 92
Handy, J & N 1 1 118
Handy, L 1 1 161
Harbour, K 1 1 436
Harris, O 1 1 105
Howell, R 1 1 100
Kendrick, J 1 1 115
Martin, C M 3 2 474
Slate, R & S 3 1 140
Thomas, J 1 1 38
Williams, V 1 1 165
Wood, A 2 1 275, 296, 330
Worley, L 1 1 214
Social Life Bolt, R 1 2 110, 132
Hopkins, B & E 2 1 232 3 2 172
Layman, W 1 2 868
Pilson, H 1 1 222
McAlexander, E 2 1 347, 418
Wood, E M 1 2 488, 570, 731
Weaver, N 1 1 335, 360
Social Security Clark, J M 3 1 115
Horton, L 2 1 417 2 2 210
Social Security Administration Clark, M F 2 1 215
Social Services Martin, L & C 1 1 152
Society Breakdown Foddrell, P 1 2 81
Songs-performed Foddrell, M & T 1 1 138, 360 1 2 26, 63, 273 2 1 26 3 1 52, 160, 234 3 2 161, 202, 290 4 1 35, 105
Spangler, Babe Shelor, W & A 1 1 154
Spangler, C 1 1 40 3 1 366
Spangler, C.L. ("Tump") Bolt 3 2 113
Spangler, C 1 1 40 3 1 366
Spangler, Dorn Bolt 3 2 113 101

Spangler, D 2
Terry, N R 2 1 160
Shelor, J R 2 1 93
Spangler, Harriet Spangler, C 4 2 240
Spangler, Lizzie Jessup 3 1 155
Spangler, Martha Jessup 1 2 74
Special Education Clark, M F 2 1 300
Terry, M S 1 2 139
Special Interest Groups Clark, M F 1 2 125 2 2 290
Speech Bolt, R 3 1 138
Spencer, Joe East, Gladys 1 2 629 2 1 238, 344
Carter, W C 1 2 628
Wood, E M 1 1 54
Spinning Wheels, Weaving, Flax Culler, C 1 1 148
Sports Boaz, J 1 1 122
Grady, F & L 1 2 588, 622
Hardin Reynolds E S 1 2 244
Hooker, J 1 2 254
Baseball Hopkins, B & E 4 1 25
Foddrell, P 1 2 200
Wood, G & C 2 2 250, 300
Basketball Wood, A 2 2 23, 35
Springs, Spring Houses Barnard, W 2 2 200, 213
Bolt, R 1 2 220
East, G 1 2 764, 791
Foley, R 1 1 205
Fulcher, A W 1 1 260
Fulcher, R & E 1 1 72
Kendrick, J 1 1 300
Springs Wood, E M 1 1 113
Wood, G E 2 1 78
Square Dancing - western Cox, W 2 1 40
Square Dances Cruise, C 1 2 91 102
Shelor, J R 2 2 143
Shelor, W & A 1 1 197, 318
Thompson, M E 3 1 40
Weaver, N 1 1 360 1 2 25
Stamping Birch School Helms, A & E 1 2 35
Howell, R 1 1 181
Standard of Living - Rise In Spangler, D O 2 1 352 2 2 200
Stanley, Alma Jessup 4 1 196

Stanley, Dennis Shelor, B 2 1 339
Stanley, Dewey Jessup 4 1 196
Stanley, Gracie (Dickerson) Shelor, B 2 1 339
Stanley, Tim Barnard, W 1 2 310
Staples, Mrs. Hylton, A 1 1 420
State Highway Dept. Employees Shelor, J & C 1 1 162-210
Steam Shovels Hopkins, B & E 1 2 152
Stedman Wood, G E 1 2 535
Stedman, Mal Clifton, E N 1 1 54
Stedman, Merrill Clark, M A 1 2 223
Stedman, M.V. Hopkins, E & B 2 2 60
Stephens, Gene McKenzie, C & E 2 2 273
Steptoe, James Spangler, C 1 1 178
Stone, Herbert Hylton, A 1 2 12
Stone, R.L. Barbour 2 1 320
Stone, Smith Carter, W C 1 1 269
Stone, Stella Hodges Strock 1,2 103
Store, W G Atkins Hopkins, W 1 1 416
Story telling Strock 3 1 408
Stock Market Crash Cox, W 2 1 318
Strock, Winfield H. Strock 2 1 320, 370-414 2 2 99
Stuart, Virginia Clark, J M 2 1 351
Clark, L L 1 1 257 1 2 381
Fain, C 1 2 184
Fulcher, R & E 2 1 249
Williams, D 3 2 60, 72
Merchandising Center Clark, R L 1 2 243
Changes Weavers, G 1 1 65
Early 20th century Clark, M A 2 1 35, 300, 355
Stuart-Martinsville Busline Hooker, J 1 1 168
Stuart Town Council Hooker, J 3 2 20
Stuart- towns Thompson, M E 3 2 30, 57
Stuart - trips to Wood, G E 1 2 836
Stuart Book Club Clark, L L 1 1 451
Stuart Chair Factory Martin, L & L 1 1 160
Stuart Enterprise Kendrick, J 1 2 219
Stuart High School Hooker, J 1 1 88
Stuart Hospital East, G 2 2 733, 749, 894
History Harris, H 1 1 115, 137, 154, 176 186, 286, 276 1 2 514, 540, 546, 565 623,701,737,793,811
W C Akers Plaster, J 1 1 206

Stuart Lumber Company Fain, C 1 1 262
Helms, A & E 1 2 371
Stuart Normal School Weaver, G 1 1 75
Stuart Orchard Martin, C M 3 1 189 104
Stuart School Thompson, M E 1 1 105, 114
Stuart Streets Thompson, M E 3 2 94
Stuart Woman's Club Weaver, G 1 1 135
Sundays Culler, C 1 2 205
Foddrell, M & T 1 2 259
Handy, L 1 2 324
Harbour, K 1 2 868
Strock 1 1 222
Terry, M S 2 2 151
Williams, D 2 1 310
Williams, V 1 2 552
Surgery - history Harris, H 1 1 100,232,243,298,325 1 2 835
Sundays - Social Life Harris, O 1 1 272
Sunday Dinners Handy, J & N 1 2 50
Superstitions Hopkins, B & E 7 2 130
Slate, R & S 2 1 100
Surveyors, Surveying Harris, L 1 1 128 2 1 87
Swanson, Claude Thomas, J 1 2 323
Swimming Clark, M A 1 2 223
Fulcher, R & E 2 1 97
Hopkins, W 1 1 52
Inscore, W R 1 2 30
Sycamore Baptist Church McKenzie, C & E 2 1 34, 129, 182 2 2 42, 256
"Tacky" Parties Mitchell, I 1 1 57
Tan Bark Barnard, W 3 2 139, 151
Fain, C 1 2 74
Hopkins, W 1 1 436
Layman, W 1 1 100
McKenzie, C & E 5 2 48, 65
Martin, C M 2 1 160
Martin, L & C 1 2 810 105
Pilson, O 1 1 420
Slate, R & S 4 1 23 4 2 52
Tanning, Leather work, Barnard, W 1 2 146, 154, 163 3 2 158
Tanning Hall, D 1 2 424
Shelor, B 1 1 177

Wood, A 2 1 94
Tar Stills Hopkins, B & E 6 2 247
Tatum, (Dr.) Bentham or Benton Plaster, J 1 1 138
Tatum, Edward Grandy 1 2 556
Tatum, Ralph Hylton 1 2 12
McKenzie 4 2 75
Tatum, Robert Terry, N R 2 2 167
Taylor, Bessie Wood, G E 2 2 705
Taylor, Daniel G. McKenzie 2 1 34
Taylor, John Wood, G E 2 2 705
Fulcher, R & E 1 2 267
Taylor, W.F.B. Wood, G E 1 1 344, 390 1 2 460
Fulcher, A 1 2 287
Teachers Bolt, R 1 1 160, 219
Clark, J M 1 2 200
Clark, M A 1 2 34
Clark, M F 1 1 95
Clark, R L 1 1 78
Clifton, F 1 1 210 1 2 41
Cruise, C 1 2 22
Fain, C 1 1 70
Fulcher, A W 1 2 339
Hall, D 1 1 36
Harris, L 1 1 281, 324 2 1 270, 301
Wood, G E 2 1 178 2 2 836, 849
Worley, L 1 1 107 106
Wood, E M 1 1 80, 163
Strock 1 1 126, 386 1 2 140-305 2 1 67 3 2 190
Spangler, C 2 1 315, 330
Shelor, B 1 2 107, 165 2 1 120, 132
Roberson, W 1 1 93, 138
Rakes, O 2 2 58
Teachers Plaster, L 1 2 837
Pilson, A 2 1 281
Martin, C M 2 1 281
Hylton, A H 1 1 22, 120, 420
Houchins, M 1 2 154
Weaver, G 1 1 60, 170
Pilson, H 1 1 412
Thomas, J 1 1 198 1 2 454
Terry, N R 1 2 62, 107, 360 3 1 47

Pilson, O 1 2 830
Salaries Houchins, M 1 2 425
McKenzie, C & E 1 1 320
Pilson, O 1 2 830, 890 2 1 85
Turner, E M 1 2 280
Substitute Martin, E 1 2 711
Technology Strock 3 2 380
Telegraphs Carter, W 1 1 104, 468 2 1 335
Hooker, J 1 1 299
Telephones Clark, M A 1 2 416
East, G 2 1 189
Foley, R 1 2 128
Fulcher, R & E 2 1 363
Grady, F & L 1 1 345
Hall, P 1 2 219
Hooker, J 1 1 281 1 2 24 2 1 396
Howell, R 1 2 50
Layman, W 1 2 686
Pilson, A 1 1 401
Roberson, W 1 2 100 107
Shelor, B 2 2 407
Spangler, C 4 2 82-168
Thomas, J 1 2 45, 248
Wood, A 1 2 146
Wood, G & C 2 1 450 2 2 20
Pilson, O 1 2 556
Clifton, F 1 2 181
Television Bolt, R 2 1 31 3 1 137
Clifton, B 1 2 296
Culler, C 1 2 145
Hardin Reynolds E S 1 1 318 1 2 295
Television Harris, L 1 2 283
Hopkins, B & E 3 2 262
Howell, R 1 2 76
Hylton, B 1 1 400
Inscore, W R 2 2 300
McAlexander 2 2 126
Pilson, A 1 1 347
Shelor, J R 1 2 217
Slate, R & S 3 2 44
Spangler, D O 2 2 200

Williams, D 2 2 394
Worley, L 1 2 695 2 1 450
Stuart E S 1 2 70
Penn, B 1 2 106
Wood, G E 1 2 683
Terry, George Jessup 2 1 141
Terry, Mary Sue Terry, M S
Terry, N R 2 1 177
Clark, M F 3 1 262, 280, 295, 33?
Terry, Nathaniel C. Terry, N R 1 1 173, 1 2 312, 404
Terry, M S 1 2 371
Terry, Ruth (Dickerson) Terry, N R 2 1 177
Terry, Sally Ann (Rogers) Terry, N R 2 1 177
Terry, Tom Jessup 2 1 141 3 1 326 108
Thanksgiving Harris, L 2 1 225
Hopkins, B & E 4 1 130
Pilson, A 1 2 329
Slate, R & S 2 1 173
Thompson, M E 3 1 23
Thomas Bill Clifton, F 1 1 317
Thomas, Elizabeth McKenzie 5 2 215
Thomas, Hosea Spangler, C 4 2 33
Thomas, Marion Jessup 2 2 72
Thomas, Posey Shelor, B 2 1 187
Thomas, Tom East, Gladys 2 2 466
Thompkins, Annie D. Reynolds Wood, G E 1 1 95
Thompson, Ella Staples Harris, H P 1 2 546
Thompson, Dr. Fain, C 1 2 376
Thompson, M.E. (Murray) Thompson 3 tapes
Boaz 1 2 740
Thompson, Samuel Amos Thompson 2 2 177
Threshing Machines Hall, P 1 2 143
Wood, A 2 1 164
Thriftiness Handy, J & N 3 2 248
Tilley, Tom Thompson 3 2 120
Tilley, Virgie Lee Thompson 3 2 201
Timber
Tobacco Farming Grady, F & L 1 2 491,495,647,173,684 706,742
Clark, R 1 1 38-310 1 2 30-90
Culler, C 1 1 293, 356 1 2 113
Fulcher, R & E 1 1 375 109 1 2 33

Trapping Wood, A 2 1 77, 85
Wood, R A 1 2 264
Rabbits Grady, F & L 1 2 622
Trash Horton, L 1 2 143
Trees Slate, R & S 3 1 161
"Trinity Chorus" Penn, B 1 1 217
Trinity Church of God - services 1-4
recorded
Triplett, (the family) East, Gladys 2 2 859
TROT Valley Williams, D 2 1 50
Williams, W 1 1 67
Truck-A-Wheels Plaster, J 1 2 56
Slate, R & S 2 1 293
Trucks Clark, M A 1 1 273
Trucking Plaster, L 1 2 479, 513
Tuberculosis East, G 2 1 50
Tudor, Mrs. Maude Terry, M S 1 2 72
Tudor, Tommy Grady 1 1 72
Tudor's Orchard Fain, C 1 2 19
Martin, C M 3 1 189
Plaster, L 1 1 92
Wood, G E 1 2 646, 658, 669
Turner, Abe McKenzie 3 2 343
Turner, Crawford Harbour 1 1 196 111
Turner, Frederick Turner, J J 3 1 35
Turner, George Turner, J J 2 2 491
Turner, (Elder) John McKenzie 2 1 55
Turner, Lashowa Turner, J J 2 1 383
Turner, Lewis Turner, J J 2 1 383
Turner, Ralph Shelor, J R 2 2 367
Turner, Shady (Shaddrack) Turner, J J 2 2 530
Turnpikes Clifton, F 1 2 20
Typhoid Fever East, G 2 2 638
Shelor, J & C 3 2 86
Wood, G E 1 2 460
Underwood, Francis Shelor, J R 2 2 367
Unions (Labor Unions) Thompson, M E 1 2 294
United Elastic Company Clark, J M 3 1 270
Carolina Plant Horton, L 3 1 173, 300
J P Stevens Barnard, W 1 2 367 2 2 268
University of Houston McKenzie, C & E 1 2 147

Values Horton, L 1 2 312
Slate, R & S 4 1 199
Vesta, Virginia Clifton, F 1 1 20
Veterans Benefits Cox, W 1 1 350
Weaver, N 1 2 320
Clifton, F 1 2 88
VA Horton, L 2 2 221
Veteran's Day Martin, E 1 1 389
Veterinarians Martin, L & C 1 2 473
Foddrell, P 1 1 263
Via, Aubrey Terry, N R 3 1 214 112
Weaver, G 1 1 196
Via, Bob Thompson 1 1 248
Via, Jackson Thompson 1 1 248
Via, Jess Terry, N R 3 1 134
Weaver, G 1 1 190
Via, J.P. Terry, N R 1 1 286
Via, Jimmy Lee Terry, N R 1 2 151
Martin, E T 1 1 242 1 2 559
Via, Sally (Cooper) Terry, N R 1 1 286
Via, Willie Terry, N R 3 1 214
Via, W. King Foddrell, P 1 1
Layman 1 2 723, 790
Vietnam War Howell, R 1 1 392
Vipperman, Charlie Thomas, J 1 1 378
Vipperman, Elmer Handy, L S 1 1 84
Vipperman, Lewis Jessup 2 2 36
Vipperman, Mattie Jessup 3 1 24
Vipperman, Pat Beasley Terry, M S 2 1 80
Vipperman's Store and Mill Fain, C 1 1 160
VA East Coast Utilities Company Layman, W 1 2 624
VA Employment Commission Clark, M F 2 1 192
VA Farm Bureau Turner, E M 1 1 95
VA General Assembly Clark, M F 3 1 155, 250
VA State Highway Department Cox, W 2 1 106
Fain, C 1 2 24
Hall, D 1 1 320 113
Visiting Boaz, J 1 1 258
Clark, J M 4 1 193
Edwards, M 1 1 235
Harris, L 1 2 318

Inscore, W R 1 2 426
Kendrick, J 1 2 334
Martin, L & C 1 2 503
McKenzie, C & E 6 1 26
Martin, C & M 3 2 600, 625
Pilson, O E 2 2 808
Roberson, W 1 1 196
Shelor, J R 2 2 285
Slate, R & S 1 1 333
Wood, A 2 2 60, 212, 220
Worley, L 1 2 486
Visiting Teachers Pilson, O 2 2 515
Vocational Education Patrick County HS 1 2 161
Volunteers Clark, M F 2 2 40, 72
Women's Auxiliary Cruise, C 2 1 243
Voting Thompson, M E 1 1 40
W G Atkins Store Weaver, N 1 1 260
Wages Wood, R A 1 1 149
1930s Cox, W 2 1 210
Wagons Clark, J M 1 1 65
Walker, Harry Hopkins, E & B 5 2 253
Walker, Mary Hopkins, E & B 4 2 54 5 2 253
Walker, Mary Pilson, A 1 2
Walker, Mary (Horner) Williams, L 1 1 267
Walker, Sally Lou Hopkins, E & B 2 1 318
Pilson, A 1 2 281
Walker, Stoneman Hopkins, E & B 2 1 318
Walnuts Clark, J M 2 2 89 114
Walton, George Williams, L 1 2 71
War Boaz, J 1 2 625, 642
Rakes, O 1 1 150
Williams, V 1 2 605
Shortages Thomas, J 1 2 63
Harris, O 1 2 372
Helms, A & E 1 2 177
Hopkins, L 1 1 130
Hylton, B 1 2 176
Warts Foddrell, P 1 1 235
Jessup, L 3 2 294
Washburn, Isaac Houchins 3 1 105
Washing Martin, L & C 1 2 886

Clothes East, G 1 1 281
Foley, R 1 1 219
Fulcher, R & E 1 1 100
Grady, F & L 1 1 301, 312
Handy, J & N 3 2 48
Hopkins, B & E 3 2 23
Kendrick, J 1 1 140
Horton, L 3 2 269
Water Systems Martin, C M 3 2 527
Weather Inscore, W R 2 2 395
Forecasting Williams, D 3 1 155, 168
Weatherman, John Slate 4 2 312
Weaver, Gertrude (Wimbush) Weaver, G 1,2
Weaver, Noel Weaver, N 1,2
Weaver, Walter Green Weaver, N 1 1 50, 60, 75, 85, 100 1 2 90
Weaving Hall, P 1 2 30
Jessup, L 3 1 192, 224
Weaving Mitchell, I 1 2 375
Shelor, B 1 1 89
Shelor, J & C 4 1 170
Wood, G & C 1 1 70
Webb, Fannie Shelor, J R 2 2 110 115
Webb, Malcolm Shelor, M & C 4 1 269, 315
Webb, Tab Jessup 3 1 24
Weddings Clark, M A 1 2 109
East, G 2 1 62, 93
Foley, R 1 2 141
Harris, L 2 1 134
Hopkins, B & E 2 2 295 3 1 49
Howell, R 1 1 54
McAlexander, E 2 2 82
Penn, B 1 1 412
Strock 2 2 32, 202
Thompson, M E 1 2 316, 334
Wood, E M 1 1 54
Wood, G E 3 2 725
Worley, L 1 1 178
Serenading Thomas, J 1 2 221
Welfare Clark, M F 1 2 50, 103, 230
Spangler, D O 1 2 178, 211 2 1 168
Stuart E S 1 2 184

Turner, E M 1 2 185, 205
Williams, D 2 2 377
Well Dressing Foddrell, P 1 1 298, 316
Wells Inscore, W R 2 1 437 2 2 34
Martin, L & C 1 2 202
West, Charlie Fulcher, A 1 2 181
West, Coy Cruise, C 1 1 91
West, Eldridge Cruise, C 1 2 323
West, John Clifton, F 1 1 110
Fulcher, A 1 1 29, 49
West, John R. Fulcher, A 1 1 295
West Liberty Schools Hopkins, W 1 1 35
West, Lula Thompson 2 1 164 116
West, Mildred Ann (Taylor) Fulcher, A 1 1 144 1 2 287
West, Staunton Richard Fulcher, A 1 1 133 1 2 46 1 2 339
West, Will Thomas, J 1 2 168, 323
Cruise, C 1 2 130
Wheat Cradling Fulcher, R & E 1 1 200, 327
Hopkins, B & E 2 1 282
Threshings Barbour, A 2 2 683, 790
Fulcher, R & E 1 1 260, 300
Hopkins, B & E 2 1 296
Martin, C M 2 1 412
Pilson, O 2 2 730
Whip Saws Barnard, W 1 1 295
Whiskey, Illegal Barbour, A 2 2 380
"White Swelling" Thompson M E 3 1 355
Williams, Annie Hall, D 1 2 236
Williams Byrd's Line Hall, D 1 1 89
Williams, Callie Scott Thomas, J 1 1 198
Williams, Charlie Hall, D 1 2 285
Williams, John Thompson 2 2 246
Fain, C 1 2 419
Williams, John P. Williams, W 1 1 71
Williams, D 1 2 97
Williams, Lena L. Williams, L 3
Williams, Louella (Mrs. Charlie) Hall, D 1 1 97
Williams, Louella (Conner) Williams, V 1
Williams, Sam Hopkins, E & B 2 1 318
Williams, Virgil R. ("Beige") Terry, N R 2 2 42 117
Williams, V R 1

Fain, C 1 1 262
Williams, Virgil Roosevelt Williams, V 1
Williams, Woodrow Williams, W 1
Wilson, Alice Turner, J J 3 1 96
Wilson, Bishop Barnard, W 3 1 65
Wilson, Walter Martin, C M 1 1 180
Carter, W C 1 2 628
Wilson, Woodrow Slate 2 2 304
Pilson, O E 1 1 590
Wimbush, Georgia (Cunningham) Weaver, G 1 1 7, 75 1 1 590
Wimbush, Howard Martin, C M 2 1 432
Wimbush, (Rev) John Weaver, G 1 1 95, 113
Winters Fulcher, R & E 2 1 122
Hopkins, W 2 1 176
Thompson M E 3 1 153
Wise, Chubby Pendleton B 1 2 192
Woman History Harris, L 1 2 112, 141
Horton, L 3 2 33, 93
Howell, R 1 2 394
Kendrick, J 1 2 279
McAlexander, E 2 2 203, 261
Shelor, B 1 1 46 2 2 115, 250
Slate, R & S 2 1 335
Strock 3 1 292
Williams, D 2 2 312
Terry, M S 3 1 154
Williams, V 1 1 60
Worley, L 1 1 124
Occupations Barbour, A 2 1 410
Barnard, J 1 1 106
Barnard, W 1 2 421 3 1 126 118
Bolt, R 1 2 23 2 1 131 3 2 35
Clark, M F 2 2 118, 140
Clark, R L 1 2 285
Harris, L 1 1 79
Woman History Harris, O 1 1 121 1 2 772
Hopkins, B & E 4 2 46
Hylton, B 1 1 89
Inscore, W R 1 1 184 2 2 209, 232
Porter, P 1 1 79 2 2 44
Slate, R & S 2 2 244

Spangler, D O 1 2 274 2 1 352
Terry, M S 1 1 302 3 1 93
Turner, E M 2 2 53, 22
Suffrage Harris, L 1 2 318
Wood Types Horton, L 1 2 24
Wood Brothers Racing Team Harbour, K 1 1 150
Wood Chopping Boaz, J 1 1 22
Penn, B 1 1 153
Wood, Clay Rakes, O 2 2 22
Wood, Craft, working Martin, L & C 1 2 766
Wood, Eunice Moore Wood, E M 1
Wood, Jim Clifton F 1 1 46, 110
Wood, Lee Plaster, J 1 2 81
Wood, Products Martin, C M 2 1 298 3 2 660, 695
Wood, Thomas Shelor, J R 2 1 24
Wood Workers Shelor, J & C 4 1 269
Woods, Edgar Handy, J & N 2 1 286 119
Woods Orchard Wood, G E 1 2 598
Wood's School Clifton, F 1 2 41
Wood, G E 2 1 116
Woods, Tom (pastor) McKenzie 2 2 156
Wool Fulcher, R & E 2 1 53
Howell, R 1 1 82
Jessup, L 1 2 17 3 1 139
Work, Attitudes toward Turner, E M 1 1 24, 273
Foddrell, P 1 2 400
Horton, L 3 1 210
Slate, R & S 4 1 80
Works Progress Administration Clark, J M 3 1 33
Clark, L L 1 1 159
Harbour, K 1 2 590
Hooker, J 2 1 84
Plaster, L 1 1 162, 180
World War One - WWI Grady, F & L 1 1 367
Harris, L 2 2 228
Howell, R 1 1 348
Shelor, B 2 1 384 2 2 30, 50
Worley, L 1 1 251
World War Two - WWII Boaz, J 1 2 391
Clark, J J 1 2 71, 190
Cruise, C 2 2 96

Fain, C 1 2 123, 174
Fulcher, R & E 2 2 61
Hooker, J 2 2 225, 375
Hopkins, B & E 4 1 345
McKenzie, C & E 5 2 284
Pilson, A 2 1 3 2 2 23
Plaster, J 1 2 385
Shelor, J R 2 2 285
Slate, R & S 1 2 183
Spangler, D O 2 1 352, 422 2 2 47,53,102,119,174,200
Worley, L 1 1 47, 64, 83
Harris, L 2 2 290, 365
Plaster, L 1 2 471
Thompson, M E 2 2 98 120
Cox, W 1 1 300
Culler, C 1 2 329
Grady, E & L 1 1 394, 425
Shelor, W & A 1 2 238
Clark, M F 1 1 172
Weaver, N 1 2 134, 170, 185, 200, 220, 258, 288, 335
East, G 2 2 466, 512
Plaster, L 1 1 301, 367
Clark, R 1 2 105
Worlds Fair - 1933 Chicago Pilson, O 1 2 830
Terry, N R 3 1 111
Worth, (Col.) William Plaster, J 1 1 223
Worthington, Bill Houchins 3 1 404
Wray, Moir Turner, J J 2 1 85
Wright, Arnold Pilson, A 1 2 95
Wright, Charlie Hopkins, E & B 1 1 40
Wright, Jean Bolt 1 1 160
Wright, Mrs. Ola McKenzie 3 2 322
Wright, Pauline Pilson, A 7 1 341
Wright, Ruth Thompson 1 1 248
Wright, Walter Filmore Hopkins, E B 1 1 40
Yates, Mary Lee Wood, E M 1 1 241
Yeatts, Freddie Shelor, J R 2 1 24
Yeatts, Kiert Bolt 3 2 113
Young, Ellen Jessup 1 2 74
Young, Grover Jessup 4 2 80
Young, Josie Jessup 1 2 74

Made in the USA
Charleston, SC
26 April 2011